TAKING
CHARGE
OF PROFESSIONAL DEVELOPMENT

TAKING CHARGE

OF PROFESSIONAL DEVELOPMENT

A Practical Model for Your School

JOSEPH H. SEMADENI

Alexandria, Virginia USA

1703 N. Beauregard St. • Alexandria, VA 22311-1714 USA
Phone: 800-933-2723 or 703-578-9600 • Fax: 703-575-5400
Web site: www.ascd.org • E-mail: member@ascd.org
Author guidelines: www.ascd.org/write

Gene R. Carter, *Executive Director*; Nancy Modrak, *Publisher*; Scott Willis, *Director, Book Acquisitions & Development*; Julie Houtz, *Director, Book Editing & Production*; Darcie Russell, *Editor*; Reece Quiñones, *Senior Graphic Designer*; Mike Kalyan, *Production Manager*; Circle Graphics, *Typesetter*.

Printed in the United States of America. Cover art © 2009 by ASCD. ASCD publications present a variety of viewpoints. The views expressed or implied in this book should not be interpreted as official positions of the Association.

All Web links in this book are correct as of the publication date below but may have become inactive or otherwise modified since that time. If you notice a deactivated or changed link, please e-mail books@ascd.org with the words "Link Update" in the subject line. In your message, please specify the Web link, the book title, and the page number on which the link appears.

PAPERBACK ISBN: 978-1-4166-0885-1   ASCD product #109029   n12/09
Also available as an e-book (see Books in Print for the ISBNs)

Quantity discounts for the paperback edition only: 10–49 copies, 10%; 50+ copies, 15%; for 1,000 or more copies, call 800-933-2723, ext. 5634, or 703-575-5634. For desk copies: member@ascd.org.

Library of Congress Cataloging-in-Publication Data

Semadeni, Joseph H.
  Taking charge of professional development: a practical model for your school / Joseph H. Semadeni.
     p. cm.
  Includes bibliographical references and index.
  ISBN 978-1-4166-0885-1 (pbk. : alk. paper) 1. Teachers—In-service training.
  2. Teachers—Professional relationships. I. Title.
  LB1731.S44 2009
  370.71'55—dc22
                                                      2009031869

20 19 18 17 16 15 14 13 12 11 10 09   1 2 3 4 5 6 7 8 9 10 11 12

To all educators who are willing to challenge the status quo . . .
and then do something about it.

Taking Charge of
Professional Development:
A Practical Model for Your School

Preface

•··•

The back-and-forth motion used to plow a potato field inspired the development of television. The development of air conditioning originated by observing fog at a train station. The idea for sticky notes came while listening to a sermon in church. Fusion came to me while sitting under a tree waiting for a class on developmental supervision to begin. I was pondering the differences between teaching and administration when suddenly ideas of ways to enhance professional development flowed into my mind. After sketching a quick diagram in the back of a textbook, I hurried to class.

Since that day under the tree, I have spent hours researching the principles that have come to be known as Fusion. Ironically, the more I've studied, the more I've realized that the basic ideas that came to me within a matter of minutes are founded on sound, research-based principles. As you read this book, I invite you to compare Fusion with the latest research to see if you come to the same conclusion.

After completing my administrative endorsement, I returned to the classroom because I believe teachers play a vital role in the school improvement process, and I wanted to gain a better understanding of adult motivation from a teacher's perspective. The district where I teach is located in Star Valley, Wyoming, a rural setting nestled in the heart of the Rocky Mountains. Lincoln County School District #2 has 2,593 students and 205 teachers in five elementary schools, one middle school, and two high schools.

In 2002, our district experienced some dramatic changes. Because of declining enrollment, the decision was made to consolidate four traditional K–6 schools into K–3 and 4–6 learning centers. I was among the many teachers who were shuffled from various schools to form new staffs. Needless to say, my first year at Osmond Elementary was challenging. Conflicting personalities and teaching pedagogies created turmoil that divided our faculty. It was at this time that I shared the idea of Fusion with my principal and superintendent. The principles of Fusion coincided with what they were studying in their doctoral program, so we worked together to pilot this innovation at Osmond.

When I first presented Fusion to the faculty at Osmond Elementary, I thought teachers would immediately want to participate. I was wrong. Not only did they lack enthusiasm, but some teachers were offended by the philosophy. Cheryl Erickson and Ileene Jensen, two veteran teachers on our staff, were the first to experiment with Fusion. Their positive experience influenced six other teachers to participate. Within a matter of months, our school culture changed from a negative environment where teachers seldom spoke to one another and rarely participated in peer observation, to a professional learning community where teachers were excited to get together to discuss best practices. Over a seven-month period, faculty members participated in 256 peer observations in which we watched one another using strategies learned from *Classroom Instruction That Works: Research-Based Strategies for Increasing Student Achievement* (Marzano, Pickering, & Pollock, 2001b). A veteran teacher of over 30 years, who initially resisted Fusion, writes:

> Fusion has made me a better teacher, and I have seen the students benefit. In the past six years I have learned more proven practices in education than in the thirty years since I graduated from college. I have had the opportunity to watch good educators use these strategies, and I have had them come watch me use them. That hasn't

happened since I graduated. Yes, I have had administrators come into my classroom, but there isn't real help in their observations. The real help is in having teachers who have used these strategies help me to become good at using them with no pressure.

Once or twice each month teachers get together in groups and discuss the programs we are working on. This is extremely valuable. It hasn't been there for me in my career until Fusion.

Refining the presentation of Fusion and developing training for teacher leaders made it possible to extend this initiative to other schools. Within two years, Fusion was fully implemented in all five elementary schools in our district.

The next challenge was to see if Fusion would work at a secondary level. In 2005, several colleagues and I had the privilege of presenting Fusion to the Wyoming State House Education Committee. They were impressed with our results but were skeptical about it working at a secondary level. After much discussion, they agreed to provide the funding necessary to experiment with Fusion at Star Valley Middle School. Once again, we witnessed results similar to those at the elementary schools. Specifically, the middle school experienced a dramatic increase in peer observation, collaboration, mastery of best practices, and teacher enthusiasm. One resource teacher states:

> Truthfully, without Fusion, I would not have stepped outside the box and implemented Venns, matrix, note taking, reciprocal teaching, and summarizing. As well, it has enhanced my area of Special Education into one inclusion program beautifully. Fusion has been an eye opener for me. I have been able to go into teachers' classrooms and see the different ways teachers use the strategies . . . a huge thank you. Fusion has opened a new dialogue in our middle school.

Three years after its start, Fusion had captured the attention of most educators in our district. High school teachers felt like they were being left out, so Fusion was expanded to include Star Valley High School. Once again, critics felt that high school teachers were too departmentalized to collaborate with and observe peers outside their content area. To complicate matters, our district had hired a new high school principal and superintendent. This development was challenging because these leaders hadn't experienced the changes we had witnessed prior to their arrival. Even with these challenges, Fusion was successfully implemented. A veteran English teacher states:

> Fusion has been one of the most positive and effective professional development opportunities to come along in years. One of the biggest benefits is the chance to collaborate and share ideas with other teachers. Fusion offers a systematic method for getting teachers together to communicate about various strategies and methodologies. Another positive outcome is the chance to watch other teachers and learn the strategies that they use to make class time more effective and efficient. I have borrowed several ideas from other teachers to keep my classroom management time to a minimum, which makes more time for instruction. Another benefit is an outgrowth of the peer observations. As other teachers observe me, I have been more aware of my implementation of these strategies. Unlike taking college classes or going to a one- or two-day professional development seminar, I am able to implement the new strategies systematically with weekly and monthly goals that our study group sets. Therefore, I make it a priority to implement these strategies. I also have follow-up to the professional development. While completing the reflective statements, I think about what I am doing, have done, and need to do. If I need advice, I seek information from the peer study group.
>
> The intrinsic and extrinsic rewards of Fusion have been a strong motivator in learning, adapting, and refining classroom management and instructional strategies for me.

Michael Fullan (1993) wisely observes, "Change is a journey not a blueprint" (p. 24). Lincoln County School District #2 has definitely had its ups and downs with the change process. The purpose of this book is to share our journey with you. Along the way, as Fullan states, "We are beginning to appreciate more of the total picture. What appears simple is not so—introducing a seemingly small change turns out to have wild consequences. What appears complex is less so—enabling a few people to work on a difficult problem produces unanticipated windfalls" (p. viii).

The beauty of Fusion is its simplicity. Applying the philosophy that the best form of professional development is to encourage teachers to learn together in professional learning communities has helped us improve teacher effectiveness and student achievement. Within seven years, teachers in our district have participated in over 4,500 peer observations and mastered nearly 2,200 instructional strategies. As teachers experiment with what they learn through Fusion, school becomes more interesting for students. This has increased students' desire and ability to learn, which has transferred into improved achievement scores. Our district is now one of the top-performing districts in the state of Wyoming. Discover how the principles of Fusion can improve your school, too.

Acknowledgments

Without the support of my superintendent, Dr. Ron Tolman, and my principal, Dr. Kelly Tolman, Fusion would still be an idea scribbled on the back page of a textbook. I am indebted to Rick Woodford for locating resources that allowed us to pilot Fusion. I would also like to express my gratitude to the board of trustees for maintaining openness to new ideas and for doing everything they can to help students succeed.

I owe much to the educators of Lincoln County School District #2 for having the courage to be the first to experiment with Fusion, especially the staff at Osmond Elementary School. We have definitely had our ups and downs, but the journey has been worthwhile. The memories we have made will be cherished for a lifetime.

I would like to thank Darcie Russell and others among the publishing staff at ASCD, for seeing the value in Fusion and for the words of encouragement. I would also like to express my sincere appreciation to Cheryl Erickson, Matt Erickson, Ileene Jensen, Dr. Kelly Tolman, and Dr. Mark Taylor for helping me with the revision process. A special thanks to Reese Jeppsen for sharing his wealth of experience with me.

On a personal note, Fusion would not have been possible without the support of my loving wife, Gaylyn. Thanks for the many hours you patiently listened to me express my enthusiasm and frustration about Fusion. And to my children, I know it hasn't been easy having a dad who is always busy. I look forward to spending more time with you. Finally, I would like to express my appreciation to my parents, Oscar and Lila Semadeni, who taught me the value of hard work, persistence, and, most importantly, faith in God.

Introduction

The Way Schools Can Be

•·······························•

Imagine a school that allows you to choose how to develop professionally, and then rewards you for improving your skills. Does this sound too good to be true? Here's how it works. A lead teacher, referred to as a *teacher facilitator*, hands out a list of best practices ranging from establishing classroom rules and procedures to initiating the latest writing program the district has adopted. You look over the list and choose four or five practices that interest you. Because you have always wanted to learn how to use reciprocal teaching, this strategy tops your list. You also choose nonlinguistic representations, metaphors, and historical investigation. For the remainder of the year, these strategies become the focus of your professional development. The facilitator gathers these papers and later organizes teachers into study groups of common interest. Four other teachers also selected reciprocal teaching, so you will meet with them in a discussion group three weeks from today. You receive a short reading assignment and a study guide to complete prior to the study group session.

Three weeks later, students are released from school two hours early. The faculty meets in the media center, where refreshments are served and room assignments are made. You pile some snacks onto a plate and follow your cohorts into Room 12, where you discuss what you have read about reciprocal teaching.

The meeting begins with a discussion leader handing out an agenda. Then teachers spend a few minutes sharing good news, appropriate jokes, and positive experiences they have had with teaching. Right away, you sense that your colleagues enjoy their jobs. Exchanging ideas about what is and what is not working in your classrooms, you discover that every teacher has good days and bad days just like you. The ideas they share, no matter how simple, are useful. Several minutes later, the group leader instigates a discussion about reciprocal teaching. Teachers refer back to the information they have read, talk about what they have learned, and ask questions about information that is unclear to them. Near the end of the discussion, the group leader hands out a short article about whales, and together you practice the steps for reciprocal teaching. After practicing the strategy, the group leader gives you a paper called "Observation/Demonstration Criteria." Basically a list of the key features of reciprocal teaching, it is designed to help teachers know what to look for when they conduct classroom observations. Reading assignments are made for the next study group session, and the meeting concludes.

The next step is for you to observe a peer using reciprocal teaching in a classroom setting. The school has gone out of its way to make peer observation as convenient as possible. A substitute has been hired to cover classes every Tuesday and Wednesday. She will cover the classes of teachers who signed up to observe their peers. Therefore, the number of classes to be covered each week will vary. To schedule an observation, all you have to do is log on to a computer network, see what time a mentor teacher is planning to model a strategy, sign up, and log off. You see that Ms. Martinez will be using reciprocal teaching from 9:20 until 10:00 next Tuesday, so you sign up to observe her (see Figure 2.2 for an example).

The following Tuesday at 9:15, the substitute comes to your classroom. You briefly review your lesson plan and then slip quietly into Ms. Martinez's classroom. The observation criteria discussed in study groups are helpful. As Ms. Martinez models different aspects of reciprocal teaching, you check these items on the observation sheet. You find that not only does this experience give you ideas about how to use reciprocal teaching, but you also learn how to get students' attention in five seconds or less using a quiet signal—something you did not anticipate learning. At the end of the lesson, you quietly exit the room and resume teaching your own students.

A week later, after experimenting with reciprocal teaching, you sign up to have a mentor come to your classroom to watch you demonstrate that you understand how to use this strategy. At first, you feel apprehensive. The thought of having a master teacher observe you seems nerve-racking. However, the mentor uses the same criteria you used when you conducted your observation. It doesn't take long to realize that reciprocal teaching is the focus of the observation, not your teaching performance. When the lesson ends, the mentor sets the observation/demonstration worksheet on the back table and leaves while you move on to a new concept. As you look over the worksheet later, you notice that it doesn't have comments or suggestions for improvement. Instead, a checkmark has been placed next to each criterion the mentor observed during the lesson. Even though your lesson wasn't perfect, you feel satisfied knowing that the purpose of peer observation is to encourage teachers to learn best practices together, not to conduct evaluations.

After demonstrating that you can use reciprocal teaching as outlined by the observation/demonstration criteria, you give the teacher facilitator a copy of the observation forms and a copy of the questions you answered while completing the reading assignment. The next day, the facilitator returns your work as well as a voucher for $50. Whenever you use reciprocal teaching to teach reading, writing, math, science, or history, you collect lesson plans and samples of student work. Within three months you gather nine samples of proficient use of reciprocal teaching across the curriculum. This documentation is worth two points, much like university credits, that can be accumulated for a permanent increase in pay.

It feels great to be part of a faculty that not only values teachers but also does everything possible to encourage them to improve.

A Question Answered

Research has clearly shown that effective teachers make a significant difference in the lives of students. In a study involving the analysis of achievement scores of more than 100,000 students across hundreds of schools, William Sanders and his colleagues (see Sanders & Horn, 1994; Wright, Horn, & Sanders, 1997) concluded, "More can be done to improve education by improving the effectiveness of teachers than by any other single factor" (Wright et al., 1997, p. 63).

If increasing teacher effectiveness is the key to improving education, why is school improvement so difficult? As a nation, we spend over $536 billion annually at all levels of government on elementary and secondary education (U.S. Department of Education [USDE], 2005). Yet these resources do not seem to impact student achievement as they should. In addition to financial resources, researchers have taken great strides in making available a variety of techniques that could greatly improve instruction. However, there seems to be a breakdown between research and the application of best practices. How can schools close the gap between knowing what's best for students and actually doing it?

An Overview of Fusion

Fusion is a systematic approach to professional development that motivates individuals to continuously learn and apply best practices. This is accomplished by making professional development as convenient as possible. Instead of expecting educators to spend thousands of dollars to further their education on their own time and at their own expense, Fusion provides time for professional development during the school day and then rewards teachers financially for the mastery of best practices. Training is a daily, ongoing process where a fellow colleague acting as a teacher facilitator ensures that someone with expertise within the school or district is always available to provide additional training and support.

The model is named Fusion for two reasons. First, *fusion* is the combining of atoms. In education, three key elements must

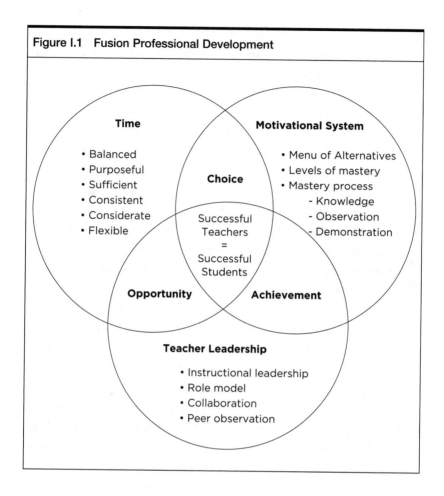

Figure I.1 Fusion Professional Development

Time
• Balanced
• Purposeful
• Sufficient
• Consistent
• Considerate
• Flexible

Choice

Motivational System
• Menu of Alternatives
• Levels of mastery
• Mastery process
  - Knowledge
  - Observation
  - Demonstration

Successful
Teachers
=
Successful
Students

Opportunity

Achievement

Teacher Leadership
• Instructional leadership
• Role model
• Collaboration
• Peer observation

be combined to promote lasting change: time, a motivational system, and teacher leadership. Second, when fusion occurs, a tremendous amount of energy is released. The combination of time, a motivational system, and teacher leadership generates the energy necessary to revolutionize education. Figure I.1 illustrates the basic philosophical ideas of Fusion.

The Philosophy of Fusion

Successful teachers equal successful students. Fusion is based on the belief that teacher achievement and student achievement are reciprocally related: successful, enthusiastic teachers are more likely to influence students to become successful, enthusiastic learners. The key to increasing student achievement is to provide positive, motivating ways to get teachers enthusiastic about education and for them to incorporate best practices into daily teaching routines.

Choice. Choice plays an essential role in adult motivation (Glickman, Gordon, & Ross-Gordon, 2004) and thus is a significant component of Fusion. Teachers are allowed to decide whether to participate and which professional development programs best meet their personal needs. Teachers also may learn new practices either individually or in study groups. Finally, teachers choose how quickly they will progress through the learning process.

Opportunity. Fusion is based on principles of adult learning (Knowles, 1980). Rather than requiring all teachers to attend every workshop offered by a school or district, Fusion's approach to professional development is individualized. Fusion encourages teachers to choose from a wide variety of research-based instructional practices that meet their individual needs and then provides the support necessary as educators work toward mastery. As a result, groups of teachers within a school may be working on a number of different professional development activities at any given time.

Achievement. Achievement is fundamental to human motivation (Herzberg, Mausner, & Snyderman, 1959). Individuals must feel a sense of achievement; otherwise, they eventually lose motivation to improve. Fusion gives teachers a sense of achievement by completing a rigorous yet rewarding mastery process that involves collaboration and peer observation.

The Elements of Fusion

Time. Educators receive time during regular contract hours to read professional literature, participate in study groups, and engage in peer observation.

Motivational system. The motivational system focuses on developing collaborative cultures within schools where teachers take personal responsibility for professional growth. Teachers choose professional development topics from a list that includes instructional strategies, classroom management techniques, technology, assessment, district programs, and guidelines for developing engaging curriculum. Teachers study research pertaining to these practices on their own, respond to writing prompts, and then meet with colleagues to discuss what they have learned.

Once teachers have gained an understanding of a research-based practice, they complete a mastery process where first they observe a colleague demonstrate its proficient use in a classroom, and then they demonstrate their own ability to use it effectively while being observed by a mentor. When they finish the mastery process, teachers are awarded a small stipend. If educators provide evidence, through documentation, that they have effectively used these practices across the curriculum, they earn points (much like university credits) that qualify for a permanent increase in pay. This process stimulates intellectual growth and enthusiasm among educators.

Teacher leadership. Fusion provides shared leadership opportunities by allowing teachers to assist principals with instructional leadership responsibilities. Teacher facilitators are chosen by their peers to take responsibility for the implementation of Fusion, while continuing to teach full-time. This element not only eases a principal's workload but also creates an environment that encourages teachers to experiment with new instructional practices.

The Improvement Process and Fusion

School reform must influence instruction, assessment, curriculum, and culture if it is to promote lasting student achievement. Many schools approach improvement efforts by focusing on curriculum or assessment without first developing teachers' willingness and capacity to work together. Beginning the improvement process with a focus on instruction (something that can be immediately changed and can influence school culture), progressing to assessment (something that is more difficult to change), and then emphasizing curriculum (something that can be very difficult to change) provides teachers with the scaffolding necessary to succeed with school improvement.

Professional development is the key to school improvement. For this reason, it must become an enjoyable, meaningful, ongoing process that motivates teachers to continually learn from one another and to consistently apply best practices. Rather than relying on a single program to meet the needs of all students, teachers must master hundreds of research-based teaching methodologies that can be applied to a wide variety of learners in various situations. To facilitate such learning across their careers, teachers participate in hundreds of peer observations and hundreds of hours of collaboration centered on improving instruction and enhancing student learning. This mastery process should commence the moment teachers begin their undergraduate studies and continue until the day they retire.

Once schools have established professional learning communities, the next step is to provide timely feedback to teachers and students through formative and summative assessment. State and district standards should be used to identify essential knowledge and skills students are expected to master. Administrators and teachers should work together to align the curriculum by developing common, rigorous formative assessments and taking an approach to goal setting that promotes student and teacher growth. This information provides schools with a body of evidence that can be used to make timely interventions.

Finally, curriculum is the heart of education. As educators master best practices and learn to use assessment more effectively, they must systematically employ these practices by integrating them into the daily classroom curriculum. They should develop engaging instructional units aligned with state standards, incorporate best practices, and provide students with in-depth, relevant learning experiences involving higher-order thinking skills.

The Fusion model is presented in the form of eight design questions. They are listed in Figure I.2.

This book is structured around three phases of school improvement. Each chapter contains scenarios designed to help the reader better comprehend important principles of Fusion. The names of individuals and schools in these scenarios are

---

Figure I.2   School Improvement Design Questions

---

1. How do you increase the morale of teachers so that they embrace new initiatives, without overwhelming the teachers and administrators with new responsibilities?

2. How do you encourage teachers to help one another develop professionally without jeopardizing interpersonal relationships?

3. How do you involve teachers in meaningful leadership opportunities without removing them from the classroom?

4. How do you provide more time and financial incentives for professional development with limited resources?

5. How can you increase teachers' expectations for themselves and for their students without allowing state tests to dominate the curriculum?

6. How do you encourage classroom teachers to provide timely interventions without neglecting a subgroup of students?

7. How do you encourage teachers to incorporate higher-order thinking activities into differentiated units of instruction without fragmenting the curriculum?

8. Are you ready to apply the principles of Fusion?

---

pseudonyms. Chapters 1 through 4 address ways to foster positive interpersonal relationships by establishing professional learning communities. These chapters describe the fundamental principles of Fusion. Chapters 5 and 6 emphasize ways to increase academic rigor through the use of formative assessment, a unique approach to goal setting, and ways to increase schoolwide consistency of student interventions. Chapter 7 describes the third phase of school improvement, which is to make learning relevant by improving classroom curriculum. Chapter 8 suggests leadership characteristics that facilitate the implementation of Fusion.

Inspiration to Change

How do you increase the morale of teachers so that they embrace new initiatives, without overwhelming the teachers and administrators with new responsibilities?

One of the greatest challenges leaders face is motivating teachers to incorporate best practices, especially tenured teachers who sometimes ignore innovations. Improving teacher effectiveness is a difficult undertaking for several reasons. Educators are already overwhelmed with social and academic responsibilities. Most educators already have developed habits of working alone instead of with colleagues, which hinders the improvement process. Experienced teachers have seen innovations come and go; therefore, they resist new programs. The format of workshops and other trainings often ignores principles of adult learning, making it difficult to internalize new information. The public educational system is structured in such a way that educators, regardless of their effectiveness, receive the same recognition and pay as their colleagues. As a result, enthusiastic teachers gradually lose motivation to improve.

Scenario

Mr. Rodriguez is a principal at Cedar Ridge Middle School. Test scores in language arts and math have not improved in the past two years. Fearing that his school might be placed on the district's list of schools in need of improvement, he feels pressured to make some changes, so he visits several high-performing schools to learn more about their programs. He also spends hours applying for grants that would allow his school to adopt several of these programs. Wanting to provide his teachers with the best training possible, Mr. Rodriguez arranges for presenters from several companies to come to his school at the beginning of the year and introduce new ways of teaching reading, writing, and math. Because the district has placed a strong emphasis on curricular integration, all teachers are required to attend the workshops, regardless of what they teach.

Mr. Rodriguez enthusiastically greets his teachers as they arrive for the first workshop; however, many of these teachers do not share his enthusiasm. Comments such as "Here we go again!" and "Why do we have to do this?" are overheard as teachers shuffle to their seats (nontenured teachers up front and experienced teachers near the back where they can carry on quiet conversations throughout the training).

Over the next three days, one of two things happens. Some of the presenters share enormous amounts of information, requiring teachers to flip quickly through piles of resource materials. Other presenters offer little or no insight. Much to his dismay, Mr. Rodriguez notices that his teachers' morale seems to deteriorate with each passing day. However, he reassures himself that once the school year gets under way they will find time to read the materials provided by the training and incorporate these new programs.

Several months later, Mr. Rodriguez notices that most of the training resources sit unopened on teachers' shelves. Even those who were excited at the time of the training aren't implementing the programs. With constant threats and reminders, Mr. Rodriguez can get his teachers to use bits and pieces of the training, but once he stops pestering them, they continue with the same routines they have used for years.

Theory

Professional development must include three important components to be meaningful: (1) all training activities should incorporate principles of adult learning; (2) professional development ought to provide teachers with multiple, varied exposures to new information; and (3) staff development should encourage teachers to practice new skills until they can apply what they have learned.

Application of principles of adult learning increases the productivity of professional development. The theory of andragogy, popularized in the United States by Malcolm Knowles (1980), proposes several basic assumptions about adult learning:

• **Adults need to be self-directing.** Autonomy is fundamental to adult learning. Allowing teachers to choose professional development of personal interest increases the likelihood that they will transfer newfound knowledge into classroom instruction. However, the degree of teacher autonomy should equal their developmental needs as discussed in Chapter 3.

• **Adults have accumulated a vast reservoir of life experiences that should be tapped throughout the learning process.** Teachers value the experience they have gained through years of teaching. Ignoring these experiences can lead to resistance, defensiveness, or withdrawal from the learning activity. Thus, the more effectively innovations are linked to teachers' previous experiences, the more likely they will accept new practices. Collaboration, when used appropriately, can help teachers make this connection. Because adults rely heavily on past experiences to learn new information, it is unrealistic to expect teachers to abandon everything they have previously used to fully and completely embrace new innovations. As a result, strategies implemented by teachers are seldom identical to the way strategies were originally presented.

• **Adults learn when they feel a need to learn.** Knowles (1972) explains, "The adult . . . comes into an educational activity largely because he is experiencing some inadequacy in coping with current life problems" (p. 36). Unless educators feel dissatisfied with some aspect of their teaching performance, chances are good they will not feel a need to learn something new. The secret to success is helping educators develop a strong desire or need to learn without discouraging them. Assessment and evaluation, when used appropriately, can create this need.

• **Adults are performance centered.** For this reason, they are interested in learning practical information that can be applied to help them solve real-life problems. When planning professional development, ensure that each training session provides meaningful strategies that can be applied immediately; otherwise, teachers are unlikely to transfer what they learn to the classroom.

• **Adult learning is primarily intrinsically motivated** (Knowles, 1984). Teacher participation in learning activities is based on personal needs rather than externally imposed requirements to encourage teacher participation. According to Stephen Brookfield (1986), intimidation or coercion has no place in motivating adult participation.

In summary, the ideal learning environment for teachers is one that values individual professional expertise, allowing them to choose practical strategies of personal interest that can be immediately applied to solve problems in the classroom.

Individuals learn and retain information when the learning process involves multiple and varied exposures to content over a fairly short period of time (Nuthall, 1999; Nuthall & Alton-Lee, 1995; Rovee-Collier, 1995). Rather than presenting excessive information through one-shot workshops, professional development should be a daily, ongoing process in which teachers study small amounts of information in detail and then apply this information multiple times in a variety of circumstances.

Practice bridges the gap between knowledge and application. According to Marzano, Pickering, and Pollock (2001b), individuals need to practice a new skill about 24 times before they reach 80 percent competency. Professional development must be presented in a manner that provides teachers with multiple opportunities to practice new strategies, in order to reach a level of competency where teachers feel comfortable applying what they have learned.

Implementing Fusion

Step 1: Identify best practices.

The motivational system of Fusion is based on the pursuit of best practices. The use of *effect size* can be helpful to schools when determining the effectiveness of instructional techniques. "An effect size expresses the increase or decrease in achievement of the experimental group (the group of students who are exposed to a specific instructional technique) in standard deviation units" (Marzano et al., 2001b, p. 4). Researcher Jacob Cohen (1988) explains that an effect size of 0.20 can be considered small, an effect size of 0.50 can be considered medium, and an effect size of 0.80 can be considered large (pp. 25–26).

Although it is important to use research to identify best practices, many exceptional teachers use effective strategies that perhaps have not been researched to the extent that an effect size has been determined. Disregarding these practices for the lack of a formal research base would do a great disservice to education. Therefore, use common sense as well as formal research when identifying best practices.

Step 2: Provide teachers with a Menu of Alternatives.

As best practices are identified, place them in categories (see Figure 1.1). The Menu of Alternatives is meant to be versatile. Schools are encouraged to add or eliminate practices or categories based on methodologies schools value.

Strategies are single instructional techniques that facilitate the learning process. They generally are simple and straightforward. For example, the Venn diagram is a strategy that enhances learning.

> Mike has been teaching for 20 years. He would like to refine his skills by learning how to use metaphors to teach content. At the beginning of the school year, he chooses "Metaphors" from the Menu of Alternatives. Throughout the year, as teachers participate in Fusion, Mike learns how to incorporate metaphors into his instruction.

Figure 1.1 Menu of Alternatives

Strategies Level 1: $50 Level 2: 2 points	Venn diagram Reciprocal teaching Decision making Making connections Determining importance
Management Level 1: $75 Level 2: 3 points	Rules and procedures Carrying out discipline actions Teacher and student relationships Maintaining an appropriate mental set
Technology Level 1: $100 Level 2: 4 points	Activstudio Podcasts PowerPoint
Approaches Level 1: $300 Level 2: 12 points	Identifying similarities and differences Reinforcing effort and providing recognition Nonlinguistic representation Sustained Silent Reading
Assessment Level 1: $200 Level 2: 8 points	Pre- and post-test Periodic assessments Teacher goals Student goals Student binders
Programs Level 1: $400 Level 2: 16 points	Accelerated Math Reading Renaissance Rebecca Sitton Spelling Writing Workshop
Curriculum Level 1: $500 Level 2: 20 points	Enhance personal knowledge Deliver quality instruction Measure student progress Organize unit binder

Any technique or mannerism used by teachers to maintain safe, comfortable, and orderly environments that preserve the dignity of students, promote high expectations, and maximize on-task behavior would be placed under classroom *management*.

> Megan is a first-year teacher. Similar to other new teachers, she struggles with classroom management issues. Her principal has advised her to learn more about classroom procedures. Megan selects "Rules and Procedures" from the Menu of Alternatives and then studies *How to Be an Effective Teacher the First Days of School* (Wong & Wong, 2005) to learn how to better manage her classroom.

Technology is divided into two subcategories, the first being teacher centered. A teacher-centered focus on technology encourages competency in the use of word processing, spreadsheets, computerized grading systems, and other sources of technology that facilitate or enhance teachers' ability to meet student needs.

> Gwen would like to incorporate the use of technology into her instruction but doesn't know where to begin. Her principal recently purchased interactive whiteboards for every teacher in the school and has encouraged Gwen to learn how to use this technology. To accomplish this goal, she chooses Activstudio (Pearce, 2009) from the Menu of Alternatives and uses Fusion to help her learn the basics of this software.

The second technology focus is student centered, helping students use technology to facilitate learning. Teaching students how to develop multimedia presentations is an example of a student-centered focus on technology.

> Stephen has been using Activstudio for two years now. He feels comfortable with his personal competence but would like his students to learn how to use the interactive whiteboard. Stephen sets a goal to teach his students how to use Activstudio to refine their thinking of important concepts presented in class.

Approaches are a combination of two or more strategies used to facilitate the learning process. For example, Identifying Similarities and Differences (Marzano et al., 2001b) is considered an approach to instruction because it contains four strategies: comparing, classifying, metaphors, and analogies. Expertise in each of these strategies is necessary for teachers to truly understand the Identifying Similarities and Differences approach to instruction.

> Becky is an English teacher who wants to enhance her ability to teach students how to summarize information and take notes. For this reason, she decides to focus on mastering summarizing and note taking (Marzano et al., 2001b). Her goal is to learn combination note taking, rule-based summarizing, and reciprocal teaching—strategies that will improve her students' ability to summarize information.

Effective use of formative and summative *assessment* is a crucial part of education. Formative assessment encourages teachers to closely monitor student progress throughout the learning process, whereas summative assessment determines student competence at the conclusion of a learning experience. Chapter 5 suggests ways educators can increase the productivity of assessment.

> Raul is a veteran teacher who wants to better prepare his students for state tests. He decides that aligning formative assessment with state standards will help him monitor student progress more effectively. Therefore, he selects "Assessment" from the Menu of Alternatives and uses Fusion to help him accomplish this goal.

Commercial *programs,* adopted by schools or districts to target a specific content area, are another category on the Menu of Alternatives. For example, Writing Workshop (Calkins & Martinelli, 2006) is a program that focuses on the specific content area of writing. Programs can be quite complex, requiring great amounts of effort on the teachers' part to learn and implement them.

> Springville Elementary School has recently adopted the Rebecca Sitton Spelling program (Sitton, 2006). The principal has made it clear that he wants every teacher to use this program with fidelity. For this reason, the faculty makes Rebecca Sitton the focus of professional development and uses Fusion to learn this program.

Curriculum refers to the development of organized units of instruction that make education relevant to students. Chapter 7 provides guidelines on ways teachers can enhance their personal knowledge of their content area, develop curriculum that corresponds with state and district standards, deliver instruction that engages students in higher levels of Bloom's taxonomy (Bloom, 1956), measure student progress, and organize resources into unit binders that can be used throughout teachers' careers.

> Peggy and Rita are 6th grade teachers and have been involved with Fusion for the past four years. They have reached a point where they would like to integrate the strategies they have learned into thematic units of instruction. Therefore, Peggy and Rita's focus for this year is to use time devoted to Fusion to collaboratively develop a unit that is aligned with state standards, incorporates the practices they have learned, and engages students in higher levels of Bloom's taxonomy. Much of their professional development time will be spent searching for high-quality resources and organizing this information into a format they can use from year to year.

Step 3: Encourage teachers to experiment with best practices.

The motivational system of Fusion is divided into two levels of mastery. Level 1 exposes teachers to new instructional practices in a nonthreatening manner.

Fear of failure prevents many individuals, especially adults, from trying new things. For example, adults who have never played basketball more than likely will not join a city basketball league simply because they do not want to embarrass themselves in front of their peers. A similar attitude prevails for teachers who believe attempting new instructional practices means possible failure. For this reason, the purpose of Level 1 is to encourage teachers to take risks by experimenting with new teaching methods in a nonthreatening environment. Teachers with absolutely no summative authority—that is, power to fire, give raises, and so forth—oversee Fusion. This approach takes much of the threat out of peer observation. Also, realistic expectations prevent teachers from experiencing failure. As long as teachers have practiced an instructional strategy several times and can demonstrate a basic level of proficiency, they have completed Level 1. Finally, after finishing Level 1, teachers are rewarded with a one-time stipend based on the category of the instructional practice.

Paying teachers a stipend on completion of Level 1 is important. Not all teachers are motivated by money, but many are. The stipend acts as an external motivator to encourage teachers, even hard-to-motivate ones, to experiment with new instructional practices they otherwise would not attempt to learn. Also, similar to how a long-distance runner feels when crossing the finish line at the end of a challenging race, the stipend helps teachers feel a sense of achievement and satisfaction after learning a new instructional practice. This sense of closure is rewarding and motivates teachers to repeat the learning process. Finally, what better way is there to upgrade education than to reward teachers for improving their teaching skills? Rewarding ambitious teachers who continue to develop professionally provides schools with an incentive to attract and retain excellent teachers. Figure 1.1 (p. 16) shows the Menu of Alternatives with stipends assigned to each category. The amounts listed are for illustrative purposes; the amount of the stipend for each category may vary from district to district as long as it motivates teachers to experiment with new instructional practices without becoming too much of a financial burden.

On completion of the mastery process (described in Chapter 2), Mike would earn $50 for learning how to use metaphors to teach content, Megan would earn $75 for establishing classroom procedures, Gwen and Stephen would each earn $100 for becoming proficient with different aspects of Activstudio, Raul would earn $200 for successfully integrating formative assessment into his daily instruction, Becky would earn $300 for learning how to use Summarizing and Note Taking, teachers at Springville Elementary would each earn $400 for proficient use of the spelling program, and Peggy and Rita would each earn $500 for developing and incorporating a thematic unit that differentiates instruction and engages students in higher levels of Bloom's taxonomy.

Step 4: Encourage teachers to master best practices.

The purpose of Level 2 is to encourage teachers to refine their skills by using an instructional practice multiple times across the curriculum. To complete Level 2, teachers provide samples of student work or lesson plans that demonstrate the effective use of an instructional practice three times in three content areas for a total of nine times. Teachers who teach only one subject collect nine different samples within their content area. Each sample must include a brief teacher reflection stating what went well with the lesson as well as what they will do differently next time to improve their performance.

On completing Level 2, teachers earn points that are added together to earn a permanent increase in pay. Teachers earn 20 points for developing a quality unit, 16 points for mastery of a program, 12 points for the mastery of an approach, 8 points for effective use of assessment, 4 points for mastery of district-approved technology, 3 points for the mastery of a classroom management technique, and 2 points for mastery of an instructional strategy. To qualify for a permanent increase in pay, teachers must earn 65 points by mastering an instructional practice from each category on the Menu of Alternatives, and then earn another 10 points by learning additional instructional practices of personal interest for a total of 75 points.

After finishing Level 2, the teacher meets individually with the building administrator and the teacher facilitator to share her work. The principal and facilitator evaluate the teacher's samples of proficiency that have been collected in binders. The principal or facilitator may also ask the teacher to demonstrate any one of the instructional practices she claims to have mastered to ensure that true mastery has been attained. Once the principal and teacher facilitator determine that the criteria for Level 2 have been met, as outlined in Appendix A, the teacher qualifies for a salary change, regardless of where he or she stands on the pay scale.

Allowing new teachers to increase their salary by improving their effectiveness, rather than looking for secondary employment, helps develop and retain great teachers. Permitting experienced teachers who have reached the top of the pay scale to advance financially and professionally rekindles a passion for teaching. This process also motivates tenured teachers to share their wealth of expertise with others. Furthermore, leaders can feel confident knowing that when teachers advance on the pay scale through Fusion, they are learning best practices, whereas teachers taking traditional courses may or may not improve their teaching ability. Figure 1.1 (p. 16) shows a sample Menu of Alternatives with points assigned to each category.

Step 5: Incorporate Fusion into the traditional pay scale.

Districts can integrate Fusion into an existing pay scale in several ways. The first option is to allow teachers to advance financially as they have traditionally, through years of experience or by earning advanced degrees. The second option is for teachers to earn 75 points through Fusion. The third option combines the traditional pay scale with Fusion. Five points earned through Fusion is equivalent to one college credit. For example, let's say a teacher has earned 10 college credits but needs 15 to advance on the pay scale. However, due to circumstances, this teacher is unable to take university courses to earn the remaining five credits. Rather than becoming stagnant, he could earn 25 points through Fusion, which would be equivalent to five credit hours. Combining points earned through Fusion with the existing 10 credits would qualify this teacher for a permanent increase in pay.

Connecting Fusion with Best Practices

Teachers enjoy Fusion because it applies principles of adult learning (Knowles, 1980). The element of choice built into Fusion makes it intrinsically motivating. Permitting teachers to choose strategies from the Menu of Alternatives allows them to be self-directing, individualizes learning, and allows them to solve real-life problems. The structure of study groups and the mastery process (see Chapter 2) is performance centered and taps teachers' reservoirs of experience.

Fusion provides teachers with multiple and varied exposures to new information (Nuthall, 1999; Nuthall & Alton-Lee, 1995; Rovee-Collier, 1995). When they complete the mastery process, teachers will have independently read research pertaining to an instructional practice, responded to writing prompts, discussed the strategy in study groups, observed a mentor using the strategy, and demonstrated proficient use of the practice.

Fusion also encourages teachers to practice what they are learning. By the time teachers complete Level 2, they will have practiced a strategy at least 10 times. At this point, teachers will understand the practice well enough to decide whether it matches their teaching style.

Fusion provides teachers with short-term successes that energize the improvement process (Schmoker, 1999). Teachers typically complete the mastery cycle for a strategy and are paid a stipend within three weeks. This time frame gives schools the energy needed for improvement efforts to succeed. Contrast this approach with most merit pay or performance-based pay systems that require teachers to wait at least one year before receiving financial incentives. What would happen if teachers waited a year to reinforce positive student behavior? There is power in distributing stipends throughout the year rather than paying one lump sum.

From Our School to Yours

How Teacher Autonomy Influenced Our School

The concept of choice caused much discussion in our district. Teachers felt strongly about choice. They appreciated the freedom to choose which strategies to study, and they enjoyed being able to progress through the mastery process at their own rate. Allowing teachers to choose whether to participate in Fusion ensured that those involved wanted to be there. It also helped avoid conflicts that often arise between teacher associations and administrators regarding the use of district funds.

Administrators viewed teacher autonomy differently. Those with a traditional leadership style didn't think it was necessary. Others felt uncomfortable allowing teachers to choose whether to participate in Fusion because they felt it would cause division within their faculty. It was also inconvenient for principals to take responsibility for teachers who chose not to get involved.

Fortunately, our principal felt comfortable with the concept of teacher autonomy. Over time his patience paid off because hard-to-motivate teachers eventually chose to get involved with Fusion, which actually freed up more time for him to participate in Fusion as well.

Adult Motivation: More Than Money

Most teachers in our district would tell you that the main reason they got involved with Fusion was for the money. However, these teachers would also tell you that after a couple of months, their motivation shifted from earning money to learning best practices. Some teachers would spend many hours, over two or three months, to earn just $50. Obviously, money was not the motivating factor; self-improvement and the influence these strategies had on students were the driving forces.

The financial aspect of Fusion is motivating to teachers because it strikes a delicate balance between external and internal motivators. Stipends and the opportunity to advance on the pay scale act as external motivators. Internal motivators include achievement, responsibility, recognition, advancement, and the possibility for growth (Herzberg, Mausner, & Snyderman, 1959). Schools must be careful not to disturb this delicate balance between external and internal motivators. For example, eliminating financial incentives once Fusion is running smoothly would disrupt the balance. Paying teachers for completing menial tasks not associated with Fusion would also destroy the motivating factor. Schools must also be careful not to associate stipends with the amount of time teachers put into learning an instructional practice. Mastery of some strategies may come quickly, others require more time, but it all balances out in the end.

The Sometimes Overwhelming Menu of Alternatives

Similar to how it is difficult to choose a flavor of ice cream among 30 options, choosing an instructional practice from hundreds of alternatives can be overwhelming. For this reason, schools should be encouraged to study the same strategies the first year they incorporate Fusion. Then, after teachers have become familiar with the mastery process, they can diversify their learning by splitting into interest groups. As mentioned in the preface, we began our studies with a book called *Classroom Instruction That Works: Research-Based Strategies for Increasing Student Achievement* (Marzano et al., 2001b). The strategies offered by Marzano and colleagues can be applied in virtually every content area and with students of all ages.

Educators must be aware that if their school decides to study the same strategies, students will receive multiple exposures to them. For example, students may see the Venn diagram in reading, writing, math, and other content areas. We even had music teachers use it to help students compare instruments and vocational teachers use it to compare types of tools. Remember, the goal of Fusion is to improve teachers' skills. If students say, "Oh, no, not the Venn diagram again!" keep in mind that the way to promote independence is for students to learn how to use these strategies to a degree that they can incorporate them on their own. So, if students complain, pat yourself on the back for helping them recognize the strategy and when to use it.

Flexibility as the Key to Productivity

Implementing Fusion at the high school posed unique challenges. Classroom management, based on the Wongs' (2005) book *How to Be an Effective Teacher the First Days of School*, was the school improvement goal for the year. Because the principal felt strongly about this goal, teachers worked together to develop observation criteria (see Chapter 2) related to classroom management strategies in this book rather than focusing on instructional strategies. This proved to be a wise decision that satisfied the principal and teachers.

Including Fusion with the Salary Scale

It took four years to convince our board of trustees to include Fusion with the salary scale. One reason they approved it had to do with our superintendent going out of his way to inform the school board about Fusion. He organized a dinner at the end of each year for board members, teachers, and principals from one or two schools. Educators used this as an opportunity to share what they were learning through Fusion as well as to share samples of student work. School board members were also invited to visit schools to gain firsthand experience with Fusion. Over time, as student test scores increased, the board agreed to allow teachers to advance one step on the pay scale through Fusion.

Scenario

Principal Rodriguez decided to change his approach to staff development. This year, he waited three weeks before starting any professional development activities, thus allowing teachers to use contract days prior to the arrival of students to make the preparations needed to get the year off to a good start. This change in schedule worked wonders as far as teachers' attitudes were concerned. Knowing that their principal understood their needs made teachers more receptive to professional development.

Mr. Rodriguez also allowed teachers to decide whether to participate in Fusion. Although he initially felt uncomfortable doing this, he noticed that it made a difference in the attitude of his faculty. Most of his teachers, after discovering they could choose what they wanted to learn and then get paid for learning it, were excited to participate. Obstinate teachers had no reason to complain. Either they could participate in Fusion with a positive attitude, or they could work with the principal to set goals and develop other plans to enhance their professional growth. The choice was theirs.

About the second week of September, the teacher facilitator handed out a Menu of Alternatives during a faculty meeting. After looking over the variety of strategies available, teachers chose several practices of personal interest and completed a goal-setting worksheet. Some teachers chose one or two strategies;

others chose five or six, depending on their personal circumstances. Mr. Rodriguez noticed that English teachers naturally selected strategies that would help them enhance reading and writing instruction, and math teachers chose skills that would help them improve student performance in math. Mr. Rodriguez was shocked to find that in a matter of minutes his teachers had professional development activities planned for the year.

The teacher facilitator gathered the goal-setting worksheets and later organized teachers with common interests into study groups. Ensuring that teachers had at least one thing in common when they got together to collaborate was a natural way to promote collegiality. The membership of groups changed from time to time throughout the year, allowing teachers to get to know peers with whom they normally didn't associate. Teachers who chose not to participate in Fusion met with Mr. Rodriguez and as a group developed a plan of action regarding what they would do to develop professionally.

With all of this in place, Cedar Ridge Middle School began its first year with Fusion. At first, Mr. Rodriguez was a bit skeptical about paying teachers stipends for learning best practices. He thought they should be willing to improve without a financial incentive; however, as the year progressed, he noticed that the motivating factor gradually shifted from earning money to learning best practices. This was evident in the new strategies he observed when conducting formal and informal evaluations. Best yet, he didn't have to pester teachers to apply what they were studying. Because teachers had chosen practices of personal interest, they didn't need someone to push them. Mr. Rodriguez also noticed that skeptical teachers who had chosen not to participate in Fusion at the beginning of the year began to express an interest as the year progressed. Because he and the teacher facilitator had been careful not to ostracize these teachers, they felt comfortable changing their minds and joining study groups. Mr. Rodriguez realized that teacher stipends were a small price to pay for the benefits his school was now reaping. After all, these same resources could have been used to purchase programs that probably would have joined the previous year's programs on the shelf.

Professional Development

*How do you encourage teachers to help one another
develop professionally without jeopardizing
interpersonal relationships?*

Isolation has become deeply entrenched in public education. Some teachers feel uncomfortable sharing effective instructional strategies, engaging in peer observation, and allowing peers to give them feedback. Of the three main reasons for this, the first has to do with the competitive culture in most schools. Publishing test scores and using them to compare the effectiveness of teachers results in educators protecting ideas that distinguish them from their peers. Some teachers have had negative experiences with collaboration; endless unprofitable discussions about educational issues cause frustration. Finally, beginning with student teaching, many educators associate the presence of other adults in the classroom with judgment and evaluation, which can be threatening (Fullan & Hargreaves, 1996). Isolation can offer a form of protection for these educators.

Scenario

Mrs. O'Dell, the principal of Oakland Elementary School, has tried everything she can think of to get her teachers to work together. Traditional committees take an enormous amount of time, and her faculty resists the decisions made. She has used faculty meetings to engage teachers in multigrade-level collaboration, but this situation devolves into teachers blaming each other for deficits in student learning. Mrs. O'Dell has coordinated schedules so that grade-level teams can meet for 40 minutes each week, but teachers discuss trivial issues for a while and then have nothing to talk about. She has tried teacher mentoring, but this only works when she pairs experienced teachers with someone new. Struggling tenured teachers, who perhaps need more help than new teachers, resent being mentored—especially by someone with less tenure.

Mrs. O'Dell has also tried to get her teachers to observe one another. Having taught many years, she is amazed by the wonderful strategies she sees during evaluations. She wishes she would have had this opportunity as a teacher. To give teachers a chance to observe one another, Mrs. O'Dell offered to hire a substitute or even cover classes herself, hoping this would spark an interest. It didn't. Teachers felt uneasy about having colleagues observe them, and they didn't want to go through the trouble of writing lesson plans for a substitute.

Hoping that teachers would eventually get over these feelings, Mrs. O'Dell continued to push the idea until several teachers reluctantly agreed to give it a try. Unfortunately, things didn't work out as planned. In some situations, teachers simply sat in a peer's classroom wondering what to look for. In other instances, teachers felt compelled to advise their colleagues of better ways to teach, which resulted in arguments about teaching pedagogies and hurt feelings.

Theory

Researchers at the University College London (UCL) discovered that areas of the brain, collectively known as the mirror neuron system, show more activity when individuals observe skills previously learned than when they see skills that are unfamiliar to them (Calvo-Merino, Glaser, Grezes, Passingham, & Haggard, 2005). In a study involving expert ballet dancers, capoeira dancers, and individuals unfamiliar with these forms of dance, participants were asked to watch short videos of either ballet or capoeira dancers performing brief dance moves. Functional magnetic resonance imaging (fMRI) was used to measure brain activity while the participants, lying perfectly still, observed different dance moves. Expert ballet dancers showed the greatest amount of brain activity while watching ballet, and capoeira dancers showed the most brain activity while observing capoeira. Dancers' brains seemed to recognize moves learned previously and appeared to simulate these moves as if the participants in this study were dancing. However, when the nonexpert dancers observed the same videos, their brains showed considerably less activity. "Our results show that this 'mirror system' integrates observed actions of others with an individual's personal motor repertoire, and suggests that the human brain understands actions by motor simulation" (Calvo-Merino et al., 2005, p. 1243).

This research on mirror neurons applies to teachers' professional development by realizing that brain activity during peer observation can be enhanced if a teacher has previously learned a skill. Therefore, encouraging a teacher to study an instructional practice and experiment with it, before observing a mentor teacher, enhances learning. In addition, because humans learn by imitating others (Iacoboni, 2008), peer observation is an effective method for learning best practices. For example, let's say a teacher struggles with having students blurt out answers. If the teacher is able to observe another teacher dealing with this off-task behavior, the teacher's mirror neurons enable him to simulate strategies modeled by the mentor as though the teacher were acting himself. Then, when this teacher returns to his classroom, he will likely imitate the behaviors observed.

Contrast this application of research with how schools typically approach teacher mentoring and professional development. Usually, the person needing assistance teaches while the mentor observes in hopes of offering feedback. As a result, the mentor's mirror neurons are activated instead of those of the teacher who needs help. Why not reverse this practice by encouraging teachers to observe mentors? Also, the lecture format normally used for staff development does not activate teachers' mirror neurons because presenters typically do not model strategies in a classroom setting. Why not modify staff development so that trainers demonstrate best practices while teaching students in a classroom setting, instead of simply talking about methodologies?

As educators work to improve the quality of professional development, they should be aware of different forms of collaboration that can support or hinder their efforts. According to Fullan and Hargreaves (1996), some forms of collaboration foster collegiality, whereas others do not:

• *Balkanization* (p. 52) occurs when small groups of teachers associate in cliques. Grade-level teams, departments, or individuals with the same personal interests interact but exclude others who do not share the same group norms. Although balkanization promotes a small degree of collegiality, it mostly fragments schools and hinders whole-school initiatives.

• *Comfortable collaboration* (p. 55) takes place when teachers share tricks, advice, or materials they feel comfortable sharing, but they avoid discussions that extend to the "wider purpose and value of what is taught and how" (p. 55). Although comfortable collaboration can help create warm, social atmospheres where teachers enjoy one another's company, avoiding difficult issues prevents lasting school improvement.

• *Contrived collegiality* (p. 57) occurs when authority figures attempt to force or manipulate teachers into working together. It is "characterized by a set of formal, specific, bureaucratic procedures to increase the attention being given to joint teacher planning, consultation and other forms of working together" (p. 58). Sometimes this form of collaboration is necessary to initiate the change process. However, if schools are not careful, contrived collegiality can prevent more enduring forms of collaboration.

In collaborative cultures, teachers are actively engaged in "a cause beyond oneself" (Glickman, Gordon, & Ross-Gordon, 2004, p. 51). In other words, teachers view themselves as members of a team working together for a common cause that cannot be accomplished independently. Collegiality occurs spontaneously, permeating the daily operations of the school:

> Collaborative cultures are to be found everywhere in the life of the school: in the gestures, jokes and glances that signal sympathy and understanding; in hard work and personal interest shown in the corridors or outside classroom doors; in birthdays, treat days and other little ceremonial celebrations; in the acceptance and inter-mixture of personal lives with professional ones; in overt praise, recognition and gratitude; and in sharing and discussion of ideas and resources. (Fullan & Hargreaves, 1996, p. 48)

Implementing Fusion

Step 1: Make a clear distinction between formative and summative roles.

Individuals naturally act differently in the presence of authority figures. Think of the last time a highway patrolman pulled up behind you. Did you alter your driving behavior? Did you tap on the brakes even if you weren't speeding? This scenario is similar to how teachers feel in the presence of administrators and peers who have been given supervisory authority. Teachers become afraid to take risks for fear of evaluation. Instead, they play it safe in an attempt to please the authority figure. For this reason, it is difficult for the same person to fulfill both formative and summative roles. How can teachers believe that a formative observation has no bearing on contract renewal, when the person conducting the observation also evaluates competence?

Perhaps the most important step schools can take to encourage teachers to participate in peer observation is to create a safe haven where teachers feel comfortable taking risks. Schools can make a clear distinction between summative and formative roles so teachers know that when administrators or peer coaches with summative authority conduct an observation, the purpose is to determine their competence. Participants need to know with certainty that peer observation conducted through Fusion has absolutely nothing to do with determining their value as a teacher or renewing their contract. Also, adults are sensitive to feedback. No matter how much positive feedback is given, teachers tend to cling to corrective feedback, which can threaten interpersonal relationships. For this reason, Fusion encourages teachers *not* to provide feedback to peers. Instead, authority figures use summative evaluation as an opportunity to offer feedback.

Step 2: Change the perception that only less experienced or incompetent teachers need mentoring.

In many schools, peer observation comes with the stigma that only incompetent or less experienced teachers need to observe peers. As a result, teacher mentoring is usually a one-way process where an experienced or master teacher tutors a novice teacher but does not receive help in return. Fusion promotes the belief that all teachers have strengths and weaknesses, regardless of how much teaching experience they have. Consequently, every teacher has something to share, as well as something to learn from their colleagues. Rather than rewarding teachers who *have become* master teachers, Fusion rewards teachers in the process of *becoming* master teachers.

Fusion is unique because instead of having one teacher expert, peer coach, or master teacher in a school, there are several. Teacher experts are chosen based on their expertise with a particular strategy rather than their overall competence as a teacher. Because all teachers have expertise, each has the potential to become a teacher expert. For example, an inexperienced teacher may struggle with classroom management, but she might have special expertise with using nonlinguistic representations (Marzano et al., 2001b). Therefore, she could become a teacher expert by modeling how to use nonlinguistic representations, even if she isn't viewed as an overall master teacher. This approach creates a reciprocal relationship between new teachers and those with more experience, and it also helps teachers appreciate the complexities of teaching and the fact that perfection is never attained in education.

Step 3: Establish a purpose for peer observation through the use of observation criteria.

Simply stated, observation criteria are the key components of an instructional practice that distinguish it from other instructional practices. When teachers develop criteria, they collaboratively decide what an individual must observe and be able to demonstrate to use an instructional practice as its author or creator intended. Figure 2.1 provides an example of criteria for the Venn diagram. The numbers represent the observation being conducted, *not* a rating scale to determine how effectively the strategy is used. For example, say a teacher is conducting a first observation of the Venn diagram. Prior to the observation, the teacher modeling the strategy circles the number "1" next to each item signifying what can be expected to be seen in the first observation. When peers come to observe, they can expect to see everything that has the "1" circled. If the teacher modeling the strategy is unable to demonstrate all of the criteria in the first observation, a second observation is scheduled, and the number "2" is circled next to each item that will be modeled in the second observation, and so on.

Observation and demonstration criteria are identical, with the exception that demonstration criteria have a box next to each item, as well as the requirements for completion of Level 2. The purpose of having boxes is to allow teacher experts to check off criteria as proficiency is demonstrated. Once each item is checked, teachers have completed Level 1 mastery and earn a stipend (see Chapter 1).

The process of developing criteria helps teachers more thoroughly internalize new information. When teachers articulate how proficient use of instructional practices should look, they engage in higher levels of thinking. Criteria make peer observation more meaningful by focusing teachers' attention on a particular instructional practice rather than on all aspects of teaching. In essence, the strategy becomes the focus, not the teacher. This is a major step when attempting to remove the threat from peer observation. Moreover, without criteria, chances are that important characteristics of an instructional practice would be overlooked. Criteria

Figure 2.1 Criteria for the Venn Diagram

Observation

Teacher Observing _____ Teacher Demonstrating _____ Date ____

Level 1:

- There is evidence of a Venn diagram
  graphic organizer 1   2   3
- The steps for comparing are reviewed
  during the activity 1   2   3
- The Venn diagram focuses on one characteristic
  (general or specific). 1   2   3
- Students use important features to compare
  similarities and differences between items 1   2   3

The teacher

- determines the *items* to be compared
  (unless the activity is student directed) 1   2   3
- determines the *characteristic* to be compared
  (unless student directed) 1   2   3
- models the expected behaviors 1   2   3
- encourages students to draw conclusions
  about what they have learned. 1   2   3
- uses a rubric to assess student learning 1   2   3

Demonstration

Teacher Observing _____ Teacher Demonstrating _____ Date ____

- ❑ There is evidence of a Venn diagram
  graphic organizer. 1   2   3
- ❑ The steps for comparing are reviewed
  during the activity 1   2   3
- ❑ The Venn diagram focuses on one characteristic
  (general or specific) 1   2   3
- ❑ Students use important features to compare
  similarities and differences between items 1   2   3

The teacher

- ❑ determines the *items* to be compared
  (unless the activity is student directed). 1   2   3
- ❑ determines the *characteristic* to be compared
  (unless student directed). 1   2   3
- ❑ models the expected behaviors 1   2   3
- ❑ encourages students to draw conclusions
  about what they have learned 1   2   3
- ❑ uses a rubric to assess student learning. 1   2   3

(*continued*)

Figure 2.1 *Continued*

Level 2:
❑ The Venn diagram has been used to teach content across the curriculum (at least three times in three content areas).
❑ The teacher expert feels confident that the teacher has an in-depth understanding of the Venn diagram and can use it to teach content effectively.

---

also help teachers know exactly what is expected of them to demonstrate mastery. Finally, criteria provide a wonderful review for teachers who have already learned an instructional practice but may have forgotten some of its key components.

Step 4: Encourage teachers to study best practices.

Teachers begin the mastery process with independent study. Educators read professional literature, watch training videos, attend workshops, or take university courses to increase their knowledge of best practices. Reading assignments are typically short, from 10 to 20 pages, so that teachers do not feel overwhelmed. As teachers study research, they respond to writing prompts that enhance their understanding, prepare them to participate in discussion groups, and provide documentation verifying they have studied the practice.

Step 5: Establish guidelines for collaborative sessions.

Establishing group norms for collaboration is an essential step schools must take to maximize the potential of discussion groups. The following guidelines have helped increase the productivity of our study group sessions:

• **Prepare for study group meetings.** Teachers are expected to have studied the reading assignment prior to study groups and to have thoughtfully responded to the writing prompts.

• **Focus on the positive.** Sometimes educators focus their attention on the negative aspects of education rather than the positive. It doesn't take long for teachers to grow weary of listening to pessimistic individuals complain. For this reason, teachers are encouraged to share their optimism instead.

- **Show sensitivity to the feelings of others.** Educators are expected to "disagree without being disagreeable." This requires individuals to respect diversity and to never gossip or talk about others behind their backs.
- **Participate without dominating the discussion.** Although the teacher facilitator or group discussion leader fosters collaboration, the best way to destroy collaboration is to have one individual dominate the discussion. The goal of study groups is for everyone to share their expertise, feelings, and insight, not just a few talkative individuals. The quality of the conversation depends on the participants in the study group, so teachers need to participate rather than expect one individual to do all of the work.
- **Maintain confidentiality.** Laws and regulations protect students with special needs. For this reason, teachers must not use specific names when sharing information. Also, the use of names labels students. Those who may cause trouble in one classroom might be model students in another. Sharing negative information could interfere with positive relationships students might have with future teachers.
- **Balance on-task and social behaviors.** The purpose of study groups is for teachers to learn from one another. This doesn't need to be a dreary process. It is okay to laugh and joke as long as having a good time doesn't consume too much time or overshadow learning meaningful strategies.

Step 6: Use study groups to expose teachers to varied instructional strategies.

In Chapter 1, I mentioned the importance of providing teachers with many varied exposures to new content. Consider the following agenda, accompanied by a brief description of what occurs in study group sessions:

- **Open with good news.** Begin on a positive note by sharing good news about life or teaching, funny stories, or jokes. Adding a social element like this to study sessions helps teachers develop enduring friendships that greatly contribute to true collaboration. Occasionally teachers may share frustrations, too. Because it is difficult for individuals to engage in higher levels of thinking when they are upset, allow teachers to share frustrations so they can be productive, but do not allow study groups to turn into gripe sessions.

• **Share ideas and discuss classroom needs.** The goal of Fusion is to develop professional learning communities that actively discuss school, classroom, and individual needs. Fusion helps develop such communities by continually inviting teachers to share ideas and discuss classroom needs. Over time, as teachers develop trust in one another, collaboration becomes more meaningful, and teachers begin to feel comfortable discussing issues that normally would not be shared.

• **Discuss the new strategy.** Teachers use professional literature and written responses to help facilitate an in-depth discussion about the instructional practice they have studied prior to the study group session.

• **Practice the strategy as a group.** There is a big difference between learning new information and applying it. Practicing new strategies as a group helps bridge this gap. For example, if the Venn diagram is the focus of a study group session, the group leader would hand out a blank graphic organizer of a Venn diagram, and participants would work together to compare and contrast two items. Notice that the group carries out the activity, not the discussion leader. We have found that when one individual presents information to others, study groups resemble miniworkshops with teachers as passive listeners.

• **Consider ways to use the new strategy across the curriculum.** Sometimes teachers have difficulty associating the usefulness of strategies across the curriculum and thus may apply a strategy in one content area while neglecting others. For example, some teachers may think the only use for the Venn diagram is to compare two characters in a story. Expand teachers' thinking by encouraging them to discuss ways to use the Venn diagram in writing (comparing narrative and expository texts), math (comparing prime and composite numbers), science (comparing plant and animal cells), history (comparing the war in Iraq with Vietnam), and music (comparing Beethoven with Mozart). Encourage teachers to discuss ways to use strategies with students of different ages. For example, using two hula hoops to form a Venn diagram and then asking kindergarten students to compare various teddy bears would help teachers of younger students visualize how they could use this strategy.

• **Review observation/demonstration criteria.** Step 3 described the important role observation criteria play in helping teachers learn new strategies. At this point, teachers review the observation/demonstration criteria for the practice they have been discussing. For example, teachers would review the information in Figure 2.1 so they would know exactly what was expected of them to demonstrate mastery of the Venn diagram. Sometimes criteria may need to be modified; for instance, some strategies, such as note taking, may need to be altered for young students. In other situations, teachers may need to work together to develop observation criteria for a strategy that hasn't been included in the Menu of Alternatives. Think of Fusion as the hard drive of a computer and best practices as software. Virtually any practice can be plugged into Fusion. This flexibility allows schools to continually incorporate new strategies into Fusion.

• **Note goals to be accomplished before the next meeting.** At the conclusion of the meeting, teachers coordinate schedules for peer observation and clarify the reading assignment for the next study group session. During the next three weeks, teachers complete the reading assignment, experiment with the strategy they have studied, observe it being used by a mentor teacher, and demonstrate proficiency.

Step 7: Establish guidelines to make peer observation a positive learning experience.

Peer observation allows teachers to experience different classroom atmospheres ranging from quiet, well-structured traditional environments to active, cooperative learning cultures where students are actively engaged in discussion. Regardless of the purpose of the observation, teachers learn subtle lessons from their peers such as new ways to deal with off-task behavior, present information, and make learning exciting for students. However, it takes courage for teachers to allow peers to come into their classrooms for observations. For this reason, it is critical that teachers are extremely sensitive to one another. If teachers ever do or say anything to offend a colleague while conducting an observation, it is highly unlikely those colleagues will participate in the future. To prevent this from happening, Fusion offers the following guidelines that can make peer observation a positive learning experience for teachers:

• **Teacher participation in peer observation is voluntary.** Choice plays an important role in making peer observation a positive experience; rather than forcing participation, Fusion invites teachers to participate. However, teachers must complete the observation process to earn financial incentives.

• **All observations are based on observation criteria.** Using observation criteria is a giant step toward taking the threat out of peer observation.

• **Teachers do not provide feedback to peers.** Fusion promotes the philosophy that every teacher has a unique teaching style and as a result does things differently. Different does not mean right or wrong. Teachers should view diversity as a learning opportunity rather than a reason to be judgmental. The purpose of an observation is to allow teachers to see the effective use of an instructional practice, not to evaluate the teaching performance or give advice to a colleague. For this reason, teachers do not provide feedback to peers; evaluation is left up to administrators. Although this advice may contradict conventional wisdom, it makes the difference between teachers looking forward to peer observation and resenting it.

• **Peer observation is never used to make summative decisions.** The clear distinction Fusion makes between formative and summative roles takes much of the threat out of peer observation. As long as these roles are not mingled or confused, and observations have absolutely no influence over contract renewal, peer observation will remain a positive experience.

- **Observations are confidential.** Teachers must never discuss another teacher's performance unless the teacher who was observed grants permission to do so. The only exception to this rule is if destructive behavior is observed—then administrators must be contacted immediately.
- **Teachers must adhere to peer observation etiquette:**

     –Abide by the Golden Rule: Never do or say anything you wouldn't want another teacher to do or say in your classroom.

     –Schedule observations in advance; never drop in unexpectedly.

     –Be punctual.

     –Remember that as an observer, you are a guest and must not distract students or the teacher in any way.

     –Remember to help students only when invited to do so by the teacher being observed.

     –Discuss questions regarding the observation at times when it will not disrupt the flow of instruction.

Step 8: Encourage teachers to practice what they have learned.

After teachers have gained knowledge of an instructional practice, observed its proficient use, and practiced it with their students, they are ready to demonstrate mastery. There are two subtle differences between observation and demonstration. In the observation process, all teachers are invited to observe a teacher who has successfully completed the mastery process. In the demonstration process, only teachers who have successfully completed the mastery process are allowed to observe.

Another difference between observation and demonstration is the role of evaluation. The observation process does not involve evaluation in the sense that the observer does not evaluate the performance of the teacher expert. However, the purpose of the demonstration process is to show mastery of an instructional practice; therefore, an evaluation of competence must be made. This does *not* mean teachers are rated on how well they can use an instructional practice (teachers are never rated in Fusion); rather, it means that teacher experts must decide whether the criteria for an instructional practice have been met. If a teacher expert feels a peer has met the criteria, then the Level 1 mastery process is complete and the teacher receives a stipend. If the teacher expert feels the criteria have not been met, the expert has a conference with the teacher and provides the support necessary to help that teacher.

Connecting Fusion with Best Practices

Fusion incorporates the use of mirroring to improve instruction (Calvo-Merino et al., 2005). Encouraging teachers to study strategies, practice them, and then observe mentors facilitates learning. Also, engaging in hundreds of peer observations throughout the course of their careers allows teachers to experience hundreds of scenarios that can improve their teaching ability.

Fusion also fosters the qualities, attitudes, and behaviors necessary to establish collaborative cultures. Making a clear distinction between formative and summative roles and adhering to collaborative norms creates an environment where collaboration occurs "on a moment-by-moment, day-by-day basis" (Fullan & Hargreaves, 1996, p. 48).

From Our School to Yours

Making Peer Observation a Positive Learning Experience

Evaluation is like going to the dentist: we know it is necessary, but we do not always look forward to it. To prevent peer observation from becoming another trip to the dentist, we took a close look at Fusion and then made sure it didn't resemble traditional evaluation. Traditional evaluation typically involves an authority figure who drops in unexpectedly or schedules a time to watch a lesson, uses her judgment to determine the quality of teaching, and then offers suggestions. To make Fusion different, we allowed teachers to decide what, when, and whom they wanted to observe. We also replaced feedback with observation criteria that focused teachers' attention on instructional strategies rather than another teacher's performance. This change in perspective took some getting used to. The natural tendency is to praise teachers for an exceptional performance or to offer suggestions when improvements can be made. However, we have found that the more teachers visit other classrooms, the more they learn from their colleagues even in the absence of feedback. Making a clear distinction between evaluation and peer observation increased the number of observations teachers participated in, which augmented their ability to mirror or learn from other teachers.

The first time I observed a master teacher on our staff with over 30 years of teaching experience, he was terrified. Although his lesson was outstanding, it was obvious he felt extremely uncomfortable with me in his classroom. I simply completed the observation form, placed it on the back table, and quietly exited the room. Within a month or two, after participating in several peer observations, this teacher opened up. From that point on, he no longer felt threatened by the presence of other teachers in his classroom. In fact, the next year he allowed five officials from the Wyoming Department of Education, who were visiting our school to learn more about Fusion, to observe him teach. It's difficult to measure the influence this teacher has had on others. I can't help but wonder what might have happened if I had critiqued his performance; he likely would not have allowed other teachers to observe him.

Scheduling Peer Observations

We use a computer network with a schedule similar to Figure 2.2 to arrange peer observations. As teachers review their lesson plans, they record when they expect to model certain strategies. Educators interested in observing simply log on to the network, sign up for the strategy they would like to observe, save the

Figure 2.2   Scheduling Peer Observation

Tuesday, October 23

Time	Demonstration	Strategy	Observation
8:05–8:40			
8:40–9:20	Susan Palopoli	Lucy Calkins Book 1 Session 4	Nancy Lee
9:20–10:00	Julia Martinez	Reciprocal teaching	
10:10–10:40	Scott Bukva	Mastering math facts	Cindy Marin
10:50–11:30	Bruce Desolett	Context clues	
12:00–12:30			
12:30–1:00			
1:00–1:30	Jennifer Gellios	Metaphors	
1:40–2:20			

Strategies You Would Like to Observe

Teacher	Strategy
Megan Jones	Note taking

changes made, and log off. The next teacher who accesses the network will see an updated schedule. Teachers interested in observing a strategy that hasn't been posted write their name under the section "Strategies You Would Like to Observe." As other teachers see this information, someone usually signs up to model the desired strategy. If someone doesn't sign up, the teacher facilitator makes arrangements for the observation to occur.

Our computer network also has a folder that contains criteria, questions, and other resources developed for Fusion. Teachers simply click on the strategy of interest and print the information they need. With more than 200 instructional practices available, and more being added each year, teachers find it more convenient to access information this way.

Conducting Multischool Peer Observation

Peer observation has been extended to involve multiple schools within our district. For example, middle school teachers wanting to learn a strategy have traveled to Osmond Elementary to observe its use and vice versa. We have also used computer networking to broadcast lessons for schools that are more than 30 miles apart. Teacher facilitators (see Chapter 3) from each school make the arrangements for multischool peer observation.

Multischool peer observation has helped teachers gain a better understanding of one another and streamline the curriculum. For example, prior to Fusion, elementary and middle school teachers tended to blame one another for deficits in student learning. Encouraging these teachers to observe one another led to a change in their perspective. Peer observation has also helped teachers better understand programs used by other schools, which can facilitate the transition process for students.

Using Study Groups to Train Faculty

Schools in our district have experimented with training several teachers and then using them to train the rest of the faculty. The facilitator conducts a study group session with five or six teachers. These teachers experiment with the instructional practice and then act as discussion leaders when the time comes to train the rest of the staff.

Using Fusion to Train Paraprofessionals

We found Fusion to be an effective way to train paraprofessionals. Title I, special education, and classroom teachers met together to collaboratively decide which strategies would be most beneficial for paraprofessionals to learn. For example, we decided Title I reading paraprofessionals needed to apply comprehension strategies described by Harvey and Goudvis (2000) when reading with students. Title I paraprofessionals, under their supervisor's direction, read the research, participated in study groups, observed a mentor, and then demonstrated the ability to use each of these strategies. At the end of the mastery process, they earned a small stipend for the strategies they mastered. This training improved the assistance students received from paraprofessionals, increased teachers' confidence in these individuals, and helped streamline classroom instruction with special services.

Recognizing Collaboration Can Be Complicated

At Osmond Elementary, we have experienced the different types of collaboration described earlier (Fullan & Hargreaves, 1996). The first year Fusion was implemented, nearly half the faculty chose not to participate, which naturally resulted in balkanization. At times, comfortable collaboration has also been a problem, especially when we tried to tackle difficult issues such as assessment and the school curriculum. Contrived collegiality has been prevalent in years of accreditation. Similar to how children have to be coaxed to eat their vegetables, teachers sometimes need coaxing to get involved with accreditation tasks.

Although we have had negative experiences with collaboration, we have also experienced the positive. At times the professional bond between teachers is so strong that we feel like family. Teachers, regardless of their content area or grade level, visit with their peers before school, during recess or lunch, and even after school to discuss strategies they are learning through Fusion. Although we work hard together, we also take time to enjoy life. Once we celebrated a colleague's "over-the-hill" 50th birthday by dressing in black, as if we were in mourning, and presenting him with a cake covered with black frosting. Another time, after a particularly challenging day, our principal called the staff to the media center. We walked into a darkened room where music played, and for 30 minutes we chatted casually while he served soft drinks and peanuts. Simple ideas like these have made work enjoyable.

It would be wonderful if once a collaborative culture were established it became permanent. For some reason, we seem to move back and forth between balkanization, comfortable collaboration, contrived collegiality, and true collegiality. We've learned firsthand that "collaborative cultures are very clearly sophisticated, and delicately balanced organizations, which is why they are difficult to achieve and even more difficult to maintain" (Fullan & Hargreaves, 1996, p. 51).

Scenario

Mrs. O'Dell is impressed with the difference she has noticed in her faculty. She can walk into one classroom and observe a study group consisting of kindergarten, 3rd, 4th, and 5th grade teachers excitedly discussing how to teach with metaphors; step into the classroom next door and see teachers from various grade levels discussing how to establish rules and procedures; and walk across the hall and observe a recent college graduate helping several experienced teachers use a digital whiteboard. Mrs. O'Dell is not only impressed with the depth of discussion taking place (and the occasional outbursts of laughter) but also amazed by the instructional dialogue that occurs outside study groups during lunch, at recess, and before and after school.

Another pleasant surprise is teachers' enthusiasm for observing one another. After several months of Fusion, teachers at Oakland Elementary have already participated in over *100* peer observations! Even better, they have done this without being pestered by the principal. It is exciting to see primary grade teachers observing the upper grades, and the upper grades observing primary grade teachers. As peers have become more aware of unique circumstances faced by each grade level, teachers have stopped criticizing one another. Mrs. O'Dell notices ideas she couldn't get teachers to share last year are naturally spilling over into various classrooms.

Wanting to get involved with Fusion, Mrs. O'Dell joined several study group sessions and even completed the mastery process. At first, she felt extremely uncomfortable modeling a strategy while being observed by a teacher. It brought back memories of the long hours she had spent preparing lesson plans, only to have things go wrong when she taught her students. However, this experience helped remind her to better appreciate what her teachers go through every day. It also strengthened the bond between this principal and her teachers because they admired her willingness to lead through example.

3

Instructional Leadership

How do you involve teachers in meaningful leadership opportunities without removing them from the classroom?

Never before has leadership been as important as it is today—and never has it been so demanding. Principals are expected to fulfill administrative and instructional leadership responsibilities. Administrative duties include safety, scheduling, evaluating, busing, compiling data, attending and conducting meetings, budgeting, disciplining, and so on. Instructional leadership emphasizes school culture, quality professional development, and ways to enhance student learning. Because administrative responsibilities normally require immediate attention, principals sometimes find themselves spending the bulk of their time performing administrative tasks at the expense of instructional leadership responsibilities. One way to solve this problem is to involve teachers with instructional leadership.

Scenario
As principal at Mount Vernon High School for the past 15 years, Mr. Velek has experienced frustration with the evaluation process. He is clearly aware of teachers' level of competence. However, he doesn't feel like he has much advice to offer effective teachers, and time restrictions prevent him from giving struggling teachers the assistance they need. As a result, he feels like he is caught in a cycle where he evaluates teachers but does little to help them improve.

In an attempt to promote teacher growth, Mr. Velek has tried to involve teachers with leadership responsibilities. Some act as department heads, others are committee chairpersons, and most recently, he has selected a teacher to become a peer coach. For the most part, these leadership opportunities have been a positive experience; however, some teachers view additional responsibilities as a punishment rather than a reward. A common complaint Mr. Velek hears is that teachers are too busy to take on something new. Even when he pays teachers a small stipend, they say the amount of money is not worth the additional hours required to fulfill leadership responsibilities. Some teacher leaders feel resented by their colleagues whenever they try to share advice. Also, the peer coach thinks she is at a disadvantage: In an attempt to provide her with the time she needs to mentor other teachers, she no longer has students of her own. This arrangement makes it difficult for her to experiment with new practices. Trying to model best practices in other classrooms has been problematic, too. For example, last week the peer coach, who happens to be an English teacher, attempted to model a strategy in a trigonometry classroom. Although she could easily use this strategy to teach language arts, the math context was challenging for her. As a result, she doubts the math teacher learned much from the observation.

Theory

Developmental supervision (Glickman et al., 2004) is a unique approach to leadership. Rather than treating all teachers the same, supervisors adjust their supervisory behaviors based on teachers' current developmental levels and the immediate situation. Teachers who have demonstrated the capacity to use their autonomy productively are allowed more freedom to choose how they develop professionally, whereas teachers who have not demonstrated such a capability are provided with more administrative structure. "The long-term goal of developmental supervision is teacher development toward a point at which teachers, facilitated by supervisors, can assume full responsibility for instructional improvement" (Glickman et al., 2004, p. 208).

Developmental supervision entails four supervisory behaviors: directive control, directive informational, collaborative, and nondirective (Glickman et al., 2004). Figure 3.1 provides an overview of developmental supervision.

Implementing Fusion

Step 1: Apply principles of developmental supervision.

The concept of developmental supervision is compatible with Fusion. Teachers function at different levels of development; therefore, supervisory behaviors should be adapted to meet individual needs. Although administrators continue to evaluate all teachers as they have in the past, teachers functioning at lower levels of development, expertise, and commitment require more attention. For this reason, principals and peer coaches with summative authority should spend more time with these individuals using directive control or directive informational behaviors (Glickman et al., 2004). Teachers who function at higher levels of development, expertise, and commitment and who choose to participate in Fusion demonstrate the capacity to act without being forced, so they do not require directive control. Under these circumstances, teacher leaders with absolutely no summative authority could use collaborative or nondirective behaviors to promote teacher growth. As teachers demonstrate the desire and ability to think and act on their own, they receive more freedom of choice. Thus, effective use of developmental supervision promotes teacher growth and creates an opportunity for teacher leadership.

Step 2: Provide teacher leadership opportunities that let effective teachers remain in the classroom.

Fusion offers teachers leadership opportunities through the roles of teacher expert and teacher facilitator.

Teacher experts are fellow colleagues who have developed special expertise with an instructional practice and thus are in a position to act as mentors. They locate and share materials that help others complete the mastery process described in Chapter 2.

Figure 3.1 Developmental Supervision

Supervisory Behavior	Directive Control	Directive Informational	Collaborative	Nondirective
Description	The administrator explains the problem to teachers and then tells them specifically what to do.	The administrator discusses the problem with teachers and then provides limited alternatives from which to choose.	The administrator shares decision-making responsibilities with teachers.	Teachers are encouraged to make decisions without being influenced by the administrator.
Purpose	To communicate expectations clearly. The administrator makes the final decision for the teacher.	To assist teachers with the decision-making process. Teachers have some freedom in what they choose.	To encourage teamwork. The administrator and teachers work together as equals to solve problems.	To support high-performing teachers as they engage in the problem-solving process.
Situations when this supervisory behavior is best used	Teachers lack knowledge, experience, awareness, and/or motivation to act on issues the leader feels are vital or in emergency situations.	Teachers are aware of the problem but are unsure of what to do and the administrator is confident she knows solutions to the problem.	Teachers and the administrator have similar degrees of knowledge and experience regarding the problem; both will be held responsible for carrying out the decision.	Teachers are highly motivated, possess the expertise necessary, and will be responsible for carrying out the decision.
Person ultimately accountable for the decision	Administrator	Administrator	Administrator and Teacher	Teacher

They also oversee the development of observation criteria that truly represent an instructional practice. Teacher experts model proficient use of an instructional practice in a classroom setting and determine when other teachers have completed Level 1 of the mastery process. Because every teacher has unique talents to share, every teacher can become an expert.

The teacher facilitator is a full-time teacher who assists the building principal with professional development by taking responsibility for the implementation of Fusion. This individual organizes study groups and facilitates study group sessions by acting as a discussion leader. Over time, as schools become familiar with the Fusion process and ready to branch out into study groups of personal interest, the facilitator ensures that each group has a discussion leader capable of engaging teachers in the collaborative process, holding them accountable for doing so.

For Fusion to be effective, it must be convenient. Scheduling peer observation can deter teacher participation if not done appropriately. It is the teacher facilitator's responsibility to simplify this process. The facilitator also promotes peer observation by modeling best practices and by identifying the expertise of other teachers, who then model instructional strategies for their colleagues.

To complete the mastery process, teachers give facilitators a copy of their written responses and a copy of completed observation and demonstration forms. Facilitators evaluate this work to determine whether the mastery process has been satisfactorily completed. If an instructional practice has been mastered, facilitators ensure that the teacher is immediately paid a stipend. If facilitators are unsure whether the mastery process has been successfully completed, they converse with the teacher or with the teacher expert to resolve their concerns.

After Fusion has been introduced to a district, inevitably some teachers will be reluctant to participate. Once they see the positive benefits of Fusion, however, they will more than likely want to get involved. As teachers express an interest in Fusion, facilitators do all they can to involve them. Also, when new teachers move into a district, it is the teacher facilitator's responsibility to provide them with additional training.

Fusion requires funding to hire substitutes, purchase books and other materials, pay stipends, and pay facilitators for handling their responsibilities. Teacher facilitators are responsible for budgeting and tracking the use of funds allocated to Fusion. They report expenditures to the building administrator each month, so that together they can ensure that the school stays within the budget set aside for Fusion.

Fusion has a built-in system of checks and balances to help maintain the program's integrity. Teacher facilitators, building principals, and district administrators approve the Menu of Alternatives offered to teachers. They also determine whether new school-developed criteria can be used for the mastery process to help ensure that only high-quality instructional practices are incorporated into Fusion. Teacher facilitators determine whether their colleagues have completed Level 1 and can earn a stipend. Administrators have the final say when determining whether teachers have met Level 2 requirements and qualify for a permanent increase in pay. Administrators are also invited to participate in study group sessions to learn with their faculty and to ensure that sound professional development takes place.

Step 3: Involve the faculty in the selection of teacher facilitators.

When schools promote the belief that one teacher is better than another and therefore deserves more recognition and financial rewards, they make it difficult for teacher leaders to complete their responsibilities. Nature can help us better understand why this is so. The survival-of-the-fittest mentality prompts a cycle in which animals continually challenge the leader of a group in an attempt for a stronger leader to take its place. As soon as a teacher is placed on a pedestal, the natural tendency is for colleagues to find this person's weaknesses rather than strengths. Once teachers begin looking for faults, they are less inclined to listen to advice provided by the teacher leader.

To avoid this cycle, every teacher should have an opportunity to participate in leadership responsibilities. Fusion encourages all teachers to become experts, and all teachers are eligible to become a facilitator. This feature levels the playing field and diminishes the "pedestal" phenomenon. Also, teacher leaders should not be permanent but instead have this responsibility for two or three years; then another colleague is given the opportunity. Such rotation prevents burnout and gives more teachers the chance to become a facilitator. Moreover, teachers and administrators are involved in the selection process of the teacher facilitator. Allowing teachers a voice in who becomes the facilitator increases support for that individual.

Step 4: Support teacher facilitators in the fulfillment of their responsibilities.

Perhaps the most important way to support teacher facilitators is to provide them with time to carry out their responsibilities. Otherwise, they may feel overwhelmed and lose the desire to serve in leadership positions. Chapter 4 suggests several ways schools can provide facilitators with time during contract hours to complete their responsibilities.

Another way to support teacher facilitators is to maintain an open dialogue between teacher leaders and administrators. At the beginning of the school year, the teacher facilitator meets with the building principal to develop a plan that includes how time devoted to Fusion will be used, which instructional practices will be the focus of study groups, and how the principal or facilitator will meet the diverse needs of teachers. As the year progresses, facilitators and principals meet at least once a month to discuss how things are going with Fusion. This discussion includes general information about strategies being mastered, expenditures, and plans for the next month's professional development activities. Teacher facilitators also share study group agendas and materials used to help teachers practice new strategies. This helps principals determine whether facilitators are succeeding as discussion leaders.

Dialogue is also used to maintain the lines of communication between teacher facilitators and district administrators. All facilitators within a district, building principals, and district administrators meet several times a year to discuss Fusion. At this time leaders approve or reject criteria that have been developed for the mastery process. Leaders also discuss which instructional practices can be used only for Level 1 mastery and which can be used for both Levels 1 and 2.

It is vital to remember that whenever facilitators communicate with administrators, they must never disclose personal information about teachers (unless destructive behaviors have been observed). All information shared is general in nature—for example, "Five teachers are working on the reciprocal teaching strategy" rather than "Mr. Hunsaker has just mastered the rule-based summarizing strategy, but he seems to have a negative attitude, and his classroom management is terrible." When facilitators share personal information about other teachers, their colleagues view them as undercover agents. Teachers become reluctant to allow facilitators into their classrooms, which destroys the purpose of Fusion. For this reason, it is imperative that administrators respect the confidentiality issue by never prodding facilitators to share personal information about other teachers. Weaknesses must always be detected through traditional evaluation, not Fusion.

To be successful, teacher leaders need to receive quality training. Imagine sending a friend with little, if any, medical experience to a hospital for a day to observe a heart surgery. Would you feel comfortable having this friend perform the same surgery on you when he returned? Schools sometimes send a principal and one or two teachers to a workshop expecting that these individuals will return with the expertise necessary to train the rest of the faculty. This expectation is unrealistic. Innovations that could make a difference often don't make it past a 10-minute summary at the next faculty meeting. If schools truly want teacher leadership to make a difference, they must be willing to provide teacher facilitators with high-quality training.

Step 5: Pay teacher leaders a substantial amount for successful completion of their responsibilities.

Fusion helps bridge the financial gap between teaching and administration by paying teacher leaders for the fulfillment of their responsibilities. Teacher experts are paid time-and-a-half for developing observation criteria for an instructional practice and for assisting other teachers with the mastery process. For example, let's say a school's focus is on improving reading, and a teacher has identified a strategy that could be added to the Menu of Alternatives. Once this teacher has located resources for teachers to study, developed observation criteria, and mastered the strategy to a degree that she can model its use to others, she receives $75 rather than $50 for becoming the expert of this practice.

Teacher facilitators are also paid for performing leadership responsibilities. When determining this amount, schools need to remember that the sum of money an individual earns sends a message about the importance of that responsibility. Paying teacher facilitators a substantial amount implies that teacher leadership is important and valued. Once schools have experienced Fusion, they will realize that teacher facilitators are well worth the investment.

Connecting Fusion with Best Practices

The role of teacher facilitator acts as a developmental bridge between the classroom and administration. Facilitators learn group process, time management, supervision, budgeting, communication, scheduling, record keeping, and other skills necessary to become successful leaders. Fusion also allows teachers who are not interested in becoming administrators to serve in leadership positions.

From Our School to Yours

Principals' Vital Role in Fusion

Without a competent caring individual in the principal's position, the task of school reform is very difficult. Reform can be initiated from outside the school or stimulated from within. But in the end, it is the principal who implements and sustains the changes through the inevitable roller coaster of euphoria and setbacks (Gerstner, Semerad, Doyle, & Johnston, 1994, p. 133).

We have definitely experienced our moments of "euphoria and setbacks." Near the end of the second year of Fusion, the synergy at Osmond was so strong that visitors often commented on the positive energy they sensed when they came to our school. Student achievement scores on state tests had improved by 17 percent in reading, 17 percent in writing, and 22 percent in math over two years. Because of this accomplishment, our school received publicity from across the state—and criticism. Some individuals viewed our enthusiasm as arrogance. We were labeled as nonconformists because we experimented with strategies that didn't come in packaged programs. Some schools felt like we were imposing our methodologies on them, when in reality we were only trying to exchange ideas. Our principal experienced tremendous pressure during this time. His willingness to support his faculty through the "roller coaster of euphoria and setbacks" made the difference in our school improvement efforts and encouraged other schools to experiment with Fusion.

How Developmental Supervision Influenced Our School

Our principal's willingness to take responsibility for teachers who weren't interested in participating in Fusion played an important role in the success of teacher leadership. In addition, rather than placing teacher facilitators in difficult circumstances by expecting them to evaluate other teachers or complete administrative tasks through Fusion, our principal handled these responsibilities. Although this may not have been a glamorous undertaking, it encouraged reserved teachers, who normally would not accept leadership positions, to become facilitators.

Selection of a Teacher Facilitator

To help us choose a teacher facilitator, we used an anonymous survey designed to measure teachers' perception of their leadership abilities and their level of interest in becoming a teacher facilitator. It also identified which faculty members other teachers believed would make good leaders.

Identification of Teacher Experts

One challenge was finding ways to involve new teachers with strategies that had been studied previously by the faculty. When two or more new teachers were hired, they could form their own study group; however, this was not possible when only one teacher joined our faculty. Although teachers who had mastered an instructional practice were willing to assist new teachers, they were not interested in repeating a study group session.

To solve this problem, we made a list that had each teacher's name on it as well as the strategies they used regularly. When new teachers came to our school and wanted to learn a certain strategy, the facilitator simply looked at this list and referred the new teacher to the expert. The teacher expert provided the reading materials, modeled the strategy, and determined when the new teacher had mastered the strategy.

Let's say Michelle is a new teacher who wants to learn how to use a strategy called Active Process Vocabulary Instruction (Rupley, Logan, & Nichols, 1998). Victor uses this strategy daily and has been assigned to be the teacher expert. The teacher facilitator looks at the list of experts, sees that Victor is responsible for this strategy, and then refers Michelle to Victor, who then acts as a mentor and determines when Michelle has mastered the strategy.

Identifying teacher experts in this manner made the facilitator's job easier and allowed our school to share expertise long after an initial training had taken place.

Scenario

Mr. Velek first heard about Fusion at a conference two years ago. The more he learned about it, the more he wanted it for his school. Knowing how difficult it can be to get high school teachers to embrace new initiatives, Mr. Velek did several things to gain their support. First, he and his colleagues worked together to provide time and resources for Fusion before presenting it to teachers.

Second, Mr. Velek and several of his teachers visited a high school that had implemented Fusion. The experience was exciting, which was a great help when it came time to share Fusion with the rest of the faculty. Third, Mr. Velek arranged to have an expert come to his school and present Fusion to his entire faculty. The presentation provided the momentum necessary to get the majority of his teachers on board. Finally, Mr. Velek involved his faculty in selecting a teacher facilitator.

Mrs. Ranshati was chosen to be the facilitator. At first, she was hesitant to accept this position because she felt overwhelmed with her teaching responsibilities. However, she soon realized that her role as facilitator didn't interfere with her teaching, nor did it require her to spend much time outside the classroom. Because Mrs. Ranshati was able to model best practices with her own students, she was away from them for perhaps 10 to 20 hours throughout the entire year—the equivalent of a two-and-a-half-day workshop, which was not an excessive amount of time.

With Fusion up and running smoothly, Mr. Velek was able to focus more of his attention on teachers who chose not to participate in Fusion as well as with struggling teachers who needed direct assistance from him. After seeing the impressive professional development Fusion offered, he decided to require all teachers to participate. This turned out to be a serious mistake; negative attitudes from those who had chosen not to get involved nearly destroyed the momentum of Fusion and placed a tremendous burden on the teacher facilitator. Realizing his mistake, Mr. Velek reversed his decision and continued to work directly with teachers who had opted not to participate in Fusion.

4

Use of Resources

*How do you provide more time and financial incentives
for professional development with limited resources?*

It has been estimated that significant improvements in education over a 20-year period could lead to as much as a 4 percent addition to the gross domestic product, or over $400 billion in today's terms (Hanushek, 2003; National Center for Education Statistics [NCES], 2002). In contrast, "high school dropouts are far more likely to be tax consumers than taxpayers, use welfare and public health services, and commit crimes. Researchers estimate that each high school dropout costs society about $209,000 over the course of his or her lifetime" (Wise, 2008, p. 9; see also Levin, Belfield, Muennig, & Rouse, 2007). Multiply this amount by the 1.2 million U.S. students who drop out of high school each year (Editorial Projects in Education, 2007), and you see that the lack of a good education can be costly.

Scenario

Ms. Lee, the 2005 Teacher of the Year for her state, was asked to take a one-year leave from her job as an 8th grade teacher and share her talents with educators across the state. As she visits schools, she notices two problems. One persistent challenge is that teacher after teacher has expressed a need for more time to prepare lesson plans, assess student work, develop classroom curriculum, and learn new practices. Having taught for more than

20 years, Ms. Lee can appreciate the amount of preparation it takes to provide high-quality instruction. The other problem is a noteworthy difference in the distribution of resources among schools. Some students are privileged to go to new schools with low student/teacher ratios and have access to many resources, whereas other students are crowded into dilapidated buildings with few resources. Ironically, the schools needing the most assistance seem to have the fewest resources. Ms. Lee wants to be helpful. What can she do to help schools maximize the usefulness of existing time and resources?

Theory

To better understand why time is necessary for improving instruction, we must understand the difference between teachers' low-level and high-level thinking tasks. Low-level thinking tasks include copying worksheets, preparing materials, grading papers, hanging bulletin boards, recording grades, and so forth. Such tasks require some thought but not the deep thinking necessary to improve instruction. High-level thinking tasks include learning best practices, developing classroom curriculum, differentiating instruction, analyzing student learning, and reflecting on the effectiveness of teaching methodologies. When teachers engage in high-level thinking tasks, they enhance student learning.

Low-level thinking tasks tend to take precedence over high-level thinking tasks. For example, teachers find it difficult to teach effective lessons unless they have prepared the necessary materials in advance. Then, as assignments are returned, teachers spend hours grading papers in an effort to provide timely feedback. The time-consuming and exhausting nature of planning, teaching, and assessing leaves teachers with little time and energy to engage in the thought processes required to improve instruction. As a result, instruction generally stays the same year after year.

To maximize teacher growth, schools need to balance the amount of time teachers receive to complete low-level and high-level thinking tasks. Teachers need traditional planning time to prepare materials and to grade assignments. Teachers also need a separate time to study research, enhance lesson plans, reflect on instructional practices, and evaluate student progress. In an effort to do this, many schools have incorporated workdays into teachers' contracts. Usually, these workdays are used for professional development activities that are concentrated at the beginning or end of the school year. However, at the start of the school year, teachers are preoccupied with preparing for the arrival of students—not with professional development. At the end of the school year, teachers' thoughts are on what they will be doing for the summer—not on professional development. As a result, teacher workdays are not as productive as they could be. Also, there is a tendency to require teachers to use their planning time for collaboration and other forms of professional development, reducing the amount of time available to complete low-level thinking tasks, which in turn can negatively affect instruction.

Time and resources are limited, so it is imperative that educators use them wisely. In an effort to be frugal, schools often waste money on temporary solutions that may be economical in the short run but can actually cost more in the long run. For example, let's say an individual builds an item out of wood and needs jigsaw blades to complete the project. Comparing two different blades, he discovers that 10 economy saw blades can be purchased for less than the price of 2 quality blades. Hoping to save money, this individual buys the blades of lesser value. Several hours later, a dissatisfied customer returns to the hardware store to purchase more blades, only this time he buys quality jigsaw blades. These turn out to be much sharper and stronger, allowing him to finish his project quickly. In an effort to save money, this man ended up spending nearly twice the amount necessary. When educators use resources for practices that do not significantly improve student learning, these resources are wasted, regardless of how cost-effective the practices may seem. Schools need to be careful with the resources they have been given.

Implementing Fusion

Step 1: Maximize the productivity of time allocated for the use of professional development.

To be productive, time set aside for professional development must be balanced, purposeful, sufficient, consistent, considerate, and flexible.

• **Balanced.** Schools need to balance the amount of time teachers are given to complete low-level and high-level thinking tasks. Teachers need traditional planning time to prepare materials, develop lesson plans, and grade assignments. They also need time to study research and to reflect on their instructional practices.

• **Purposeful.** Purposeful meetings maintain a balance between the person dimension and the task dimension (Bales, 1953). Teachers need to enjoy one another's company when they get together, or else meetings lose their appeal; this requires a social element. However, principles of adult learning (Knowles, 1980) emphasize that teachers expect to learn something from training activities that they can apply in the classroom, which requires task-oriented behaviors. To maximize the potential of staff development, teachers should enjoy getting together to accomplish meaningful tasks.

• **Sufficient.** My experience has been that teachers need at least 15 minutes each day to read and respond to professional literature, two hours every three weeks to collaborate with colleagues in study groups, two days each week to participate in peer observation, and traditional planning time (45–60 minutes each day) to prepare lesson plans and evaluate student work.

• **Consistent.** Once an amount of time has been set aside for professional development, it must remain consistent and become a routine that is never rescheduled or replaced. Also, time allocated for the use of professional development should be distributed throughout the year rather than concentrated at the beginning or end of the school year.

• **Considerate.** Teachers are often expected to attend meetings or professional development activities before school, after school, and even on weekends. "Typically, if teachers are given any time to collaborate on improvement projects, the time is offered as an add-on (after school or on Saturdays) rather than incorporated as an integral part of the school day" (DuFour & Eaker, 1998, p. 121). Respecting the fact that teachers have lives outside school can actually improve their teaching performance (Fullan & Hargreaves, 1996). This point is especially true for new teachers. Rather than overwhelming novice teachers with rigorous in-service classes or assigning them multiple preps, schools should be considerate of their developmental needs. Therefore, allocate time to teacher development during existing contract hours, not before or after.

• **Flexible.** Instead of requiring all teachers to use workdays identically, professional development should be tailored to meet individual needs. Some days teachers may need to work together to develop units of instruction or create formative assessments. At other times they may need to discuss school issues or study best practices. In addition, teachers need time simply to catch up with the myriad of tasks required of them. Flexibility is the key to productivity in education.

When teachers waste time allocated for the use of professional development, rather than punishing the entire faculty, administrators should apply principles of developmental supervision (Glickman et al., 2004) mentioned in Chapter 3. Teachers performing at the collaborative or the nondirective level of performance will likely use their time wisely; therefore, they should be allowed more freedom to use time as they deem necessary. Teachers functioning at the directive control or directive informational level may require more administrative structure to ensure proper use of time.

Step 2: Provide time during contract hours for teachers to participate in study groups.

Schools can provide teachers with time to participate in study groups without additional resources. Restructuring the school day so that students come to school two hours later than usual or go home two hours early once every three weeks are ways schools can dispense time set aside for professional development throughout the year. Stakeholders must consider the advantages and disadvantages of these approaches as well as the unique needs of elementary and secondary schools when deciding which alternative to use.

Initially, the late arrival or early release of students may inconvenience parents, especially working parents with younger children. For this reason, schools must involve parents in the decision-making process and inform the public about decisions that have been made. As long as schools dedicate this time to professional development rather than lengthy faculty meetings, and schools can prove that these study groups promote student achievement, most parents should eventually adapt to a new schedule.

Step 3: Provide at least two days each week for teachers to participate in peer observation.

Fusion frees up time for teachers to participate in peer observation by hiring a qualified professional referred to as a roaming substitute, who is readily available to cover teachers' classes with only a moment's notice. The teacher facilitator trains this individual and takes responsibility for ensuring that the roaming substitute is in the right place at the right time to enable teachers to participate in Fusion.

Various ways to free up time for peer observation are possible, but Fusion recommends three options. Regardless of which one a school chooses, facilitators must teach at least part-time. Doing so helps them learn new instructional practices, enabling them to share knowledge as well as experience with their colleagues, and stay in touch with the realities of teaching.

The first option is to have two teachers acting as facilitators team-teach one class. With this option, one teacher teaches in the morning, while the second teacher completes the role of facilitator. The teachers switch roles in the afternoon. Having two facilitators promotes team teaching and creates a model classroom where other teachers can observe effective instructional practices. Also, two facilitators are able to free up time for teachers to participate in Fusion every day of the week. Best of all, students are in contact with a certified teacher at all times. However, although team teaching may work for some teachers, many teachers would rather have their own classrooms. Team teaching may be a positive experience initially, but the relationship between teachers may deteriorate over time as they discover differences in teaching styles, classroom management techniques, and expectations. In addition, this option may be financially infeasible because of the cost of hiring an additional teacher, or it could influence schools to increase classroom size in an attempt to promote team teaching.

The second option is to hire a certified teacher to work part-time. Many individuals who hold current teaching certifications but are not employed as full-time teachers could be hired as roaming substitutes for two days a week. Teacher facilitators maintain their autonomy by having complete control over their classrooms. Also, this option is much less expensive than hiring two full-time teachers to team-teach one class. Even better, students are in contact with a certified teacher at all times. However, finding teachers to perform this role may be difficult because certified teachers may not be satisfied with part-time employment or may not want to carry out the responsibilities of substitutes.

The third option is to hire a well-qualified certified substitute to work part-time. Because the roaming substitute's role is to complete the responsibilities of a substitute (and they typically are not in a teacher's room for more than half an hour at one time), this can be an effective option as long as the substitute is someone in whom teachers have confidence. This option allows teacher facilitators to maintain their individuality, is the most cost-effective alternative, and has the potential to become a teacher-training program for individuals interested in full-time teaching. Certified substitutes are accustomed to working with various teachers and students on short notice; therefore, they are fully capable of fulfilling this role. One drawback with this option is that students are not in contact with a certified teacher at all times.

The presence of a roaming substitute allows teachers to leave their classrooms for brief periods to engage in peer observation when otherwise, they couldn't. Equally important, the roaming substitute frees up time for teacher facilitators, allowing them to complete their leadership responsibilities during school hours. In addition, a roaming substitute can provide enrichment to students. Some schools hire individuals with expertise in art, music, science, social studies, business, and so on. The substitute is encouraged to share these talents with students when they are not scheduled with Fusion.

Step 4: Use Fusion as a method to increase teacher salaries.

Increasing teacher salaries is a necessary step to attract and retain high-quality educators—especially if we want to recruit talented individuals interested in professions that are more lucrative than education. In the Fusion model, an increase in salary is directly linked to an increase in teacher effectiveness. As a result, Fusion is a motivational tool that can improve the quality of tenured and novice teachers while boosting student achievement. In addition, rewarding teachers financially for improving their skills is appealing to ambitious individuals who might not otherwise consider a career in education. Also note the majority of funds provided for Fusion go to teacher salaries, rather than to sources outside the district, making it a direct investment in teachers. Figure 4.1 illustrates that approximately 78 percent of funding allocated for Fusion is used to pay stipends and teacher facilitators (who typically teach full-time). Up to 98 percent of these resources could be used for teacher salaries if schools used the position of roaming substitute as a teacher-training tool to prepare preservice teachers for full-time employment within a district.

Step 5: Use existing resources to finance Fusion.

Generally speaking, lack of resources is not the problem in education. The United States will invest an average of $10,844 per

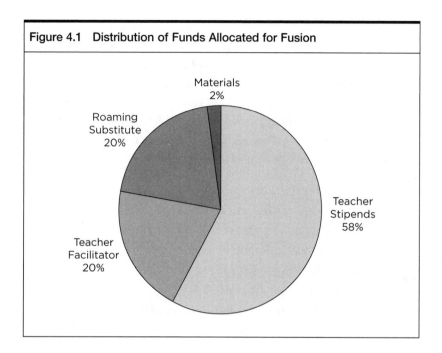

Figure 4.1   Distribution of Funds Allocated for Fusion

pupil in 2009–2010, which is more than almost any other nation in the world (NCES, 2009; USDE, 2004b). Therefore, rather than requesting additional funding to finance Fusion, educators and policy makers must first closely examine how existing resources are used at all levels of education, eliminating positions and practices that do not have a direct influence on student learning.

The first resource schools should consider when finding ways to finance Fusion is district funds allocated for staff development. Most districts set aside a percentage of their annual budget for professional development. Typically, these funds are used to hire outside experts to provide in-house training or to send educators to conferences. Some of these resources could be used to finance Fusion instead.

Federal funding is another resource schools should consider when looking for ways to finance Fusion. States and school districts have been given unprecedented flexibility in how they use federal education funds.

Under *No Child Left Behind*, states and school districts have unprecedented flexibility in how they use federal education funds.

For example, it is possible for most school districts to transfer up to 50 percent of the federal formula grant funds they receive under the Improving Teacher Quality State Grants, Educational Technology, Innovative Programs, and Safe and Drug-Free Schools programs to any one of these programs, or to their Title I program, without separate approval. This allows districts to use funds for their particular needs, such as hiring new teachers, increasing teacher pay, and improving teacher training and professional development. (USDE, 2004a, p. 1)

State and federal grants are other resources that could help schools get started with Fusion. Because Fusion incorporates instructional strategies, classroom management, technology, assessment, the development of curriculum, and peer tutoring, grants specifically designed for these purposes could be a source of Fusion funding. Most districts have full-time personnel who understand the rules and regulations of government funding and who specialize in identifying and applying for state and federal grants. Schools interested in Fusion should consult with these individuals for help in completing grant applications.

Step 6: Turn to the business community and policy makers for financial assistance.

Schools that have exhausted their resources could turn to outside sources to help finance Fusion. If the business community and policy makers seem hesitant to help, it is probably because they have already invested considerable amounts of money into education but believe this investment has not made a difference. For this reason, it is imperative that educators are extremely prepared when soliciting help from outside sources. They must present Fusion in an organized, competent fashion. Unless Fusion is viewed as a well-structured plan that is different from previous school reform efforts, business leaders and legislators will be reluctant to support it. Educators also must prove they have done everything possible to use existing resources to finance Fusion, including the elimination of positions, programs, and practices that do not improve student learning. If financial assistance from these sources comes through, educators need to express their gratitude and then, as detailed later, share results to prove that contributions made toward Fusion have made a difference.

The business community might support Fusion by sponsoring the teacher facilitator or the roaming substitute. Another option is for retired professionals interested in teaching to perform the responsibilities of a roaming substitute. In the past, lack of a teaching certification has prevented professionals in other fields from becoming educators. The role of roaming substitute could alleviate this problem because becoming a certified substitute is much quicker and less expensive than earning a teaching certification. Schools could also involve the business community by establishing a "sponsor a teacher" program in which businesses contribute to teacher stipends. For example, a business could make a pledge to support one or two teachers as they participate in Fusion. When teachers master a strategy, they could share information with their sponsor by describing the strategy they have learned and how it helps students (or how it might even apply to the business's context).

In return, the business would pay the stipend. This practice could help build a partnership between schools and the business community.

If schools want Fusion to become permanent, they must do all they can to gain the support of state legislators—and nothing is more convincing than results. The moment schools begin implementation, they should gather data on how Fusion influences school climate, professionalism, and especially student achievement. Invite policy makers to visit schools because seeing is believing. As schools demonstrate the ability to improve student learning in ways that can be measured through test scores *and* students' ability to succeed in today's workforce, policy makers will become more willing to find ways to fund Fusion permanently.

Step 7: Think big; start small.

Ideally, it is best to implement Fusion districtwide. Doing so unites schools, promotes cross-school collaboration, and prevents hurt feelings resulting from one school getting privileges that other schools don't have. If implementing Fusion districtwide is not financially feasible, begin the process with one or two schools as a pilot program. As school communities witness student growth resulting from Fusion, they will find ways to expand its use within a district.

From Our School to Yours

Getting the Most Out of Time Set Aside for Professional Development

When we first implemented Fusion at Osmond Elementary School, we held study groups every two weeks. This frequency sped up the process of developing collegiality, but soon teachers felt overwhelmed with the amount of information they were required to study. Next, we tried having study groups once a month, but teachers forgot to complete their reading assignments, and we didn't experience the same collegiality as when we met together more often. The solution was to hold study groups every three weeks. Teachers had enough time to practice what they were learning without lessening collegiality.

To accommodate teachers, we also tried holding study groups before and after school. Engaging in higher-level thinking at 6:30 in the morning was difficult for most individuals, and participants with young children found it hard to make the preparations for attendance. Meeting after school was challenging because teachers either were exhausted or rushed through study group sessions so that they could attend to responsibilities outside work.

We have discovered that Fusion is more productive in certain months of the school year than others. September, October, November, January, and February seem to be the most productive. Teachers tend to lose interest in professional development at the very beginning of the school year, when it comes time for parent-teacher conferences, just before holidays, about a month before state testing, and near the end of the school year. Sometimes Fusion picks up again in April, depending on teachers' energy level. This information can help reduce the cost of roaming substitutes.

We inform these individuals at the beginning of the school year which months they will be employed as a roaming substitute, which allows them to adjust their plans accordingly and saves the district money.

Scheduling two days per week has been sufficient for peer observation. Because Mondays and Fridays can be hectic, we originally used Tuesdays and Thursdays for Fusion. Then, once the high school came on board, we changed to Tuesdays and Wednesdays to accommodate their block schedule. Both ways have worked well. Keeping these days consistent throughout the district has made multischool peer observation and collaboration possible.

Monetary Resources Used for Fusion

Fusion has been fully implemented in our district for about $90 per student. At first, this seemed like an enormous amount of resources until we discovered that mentoring programs similar to Fusion average between $250 and $400 per student (NIET, 2009). Hiring a certified substitute rather than a full-time teacher to act as a roaming substitute helps cut costs substantially. The total average expenditure per year (averaged over six years) is $27,722 at Osmond Elementary. The following list shows the breakdown of the average annual expenditure, including benefits:

- Teacher facilitator: $6,250
- Roaming substitute: $5,237
- Teacher stipends: $15,899
- Materials: $336

Roaming Substitutes

Our district has used certified teachers and qualified substitutes as roaming substitutes, and both alternatives have worked well. Teachers typically plan peer observations so that they can teach a lesson and then have the substitute monitor seat work. Therefore, the success of this position is based more on the person's ability to work with students than the ability to present new information. To attract well-qualified individuals, we paid roaming substitutes $10 more per day than we paid regular substitutes. The small incentive helped us find talented roaming substitutes, regardless of whether they worked in an elementary or high school.

Hiring roaming substitutes with special talents was an efficient way to enrich curricula at our schools. For example, one school hired an artistic individual who in essence became the school's art teacher for a fraction of the cost of hiring a full-time teacher. Teachers logged on to the computer network (see Chapter 2), looked for times when she wasn't busy with Fusion, and then scheduled her to come to their class to teach art lessons. After four years working as a roaming substitute, she was hired as a full-time kindergarten teacher by the district.

Blending Technology Grants with Fusion

Our district has struggled with getting teachers to use new technology. Recently, the district's technology expert applied for a grant that funded training to familiarize teachers with computer software for Activstudio (Pearce, 2009), a program for an interactive, computerized whiteboard. At the same time, we developed Fusion criteria for Activstudio. Teachers from elementary and secondary schools that chose Activstudio from the Menu of Alternatives were given a training manual or accessed a tutorial at http://automiclearning.com to help them learn this program's basic features. Technology experts from each school conducted study group sessions in which they modeled how to use Activstudio and determined when teachers completed the mastery process. Our district's technology expert also offered evening courses in an attempt to better accommodate teachers.

At the end of the school year, arrangements were made to have trainers from Promethean (Pearce, 2009) come to our district to reinforce what teachers had learned. During this training, teachers received time to use the basic skills learned through Fusion to create lessons for Activstudio. Trainers answered questions and elaborated on teachers' understanding of this program. Even though this process was labor intensive, participants are incorporating Activstudio into daily instruction, which is quite a break-through for our district.

Scenario

Ms. Lee discovered Fusion while visiting schools across the state. Impressed with its efficient use of time and resources, she wanted to make Fusion available to her own faculty. She began the implementation process by sharing the concept with her building administrator. Then, she and her principal discussed Fusion with the superintendent. Gaining his support was crucial: not only did the superintendent help convince the rest of the administrative team and the school board to experiment with Fusion, but he also influenced schools to adjust their schedules, providing teachers with two hours every three weeks to participate in professional development.

The next challenge was to finance Fusion. Because her district had limited resources, the administrative team decided to pilot Fusion at Ms. Lee's school and then to gradually expand to other schools. Rather than trying to fund Fusion with one lump sum, Ms. Lee and her principal broke it down into four areas and then used different resources to finance each of these areas. For example, monies received from the district for professional development, Title II funds, and a portion of an Improving Teacher Quality Grant were used to pay teacher stipends. The director of instruction applied for and received a grant designed to hire instructional facilitators or peer coaches. These resources were used to pay the teacher facilitator. A small portion of the school's budget was used to purchase materials that would enable teachers to study best practices.

Ms. Lee and her principal considered several ways to fund the fourth area: a roaming substitute. Their school did not have enough resources to pay two full-time teachers to team-teach one class, so they decided to hire a certified substitute to work with the teacher facilitator instead. They explored the possibility of scheduling peer observation so that the roaming substitute would cover teachers' classes at times when the sub could assist Title I students with reading, which might allow the school to use Title I funds for this position. Another option was to ask local businesses to sponsor the roaming substitute. A third alternative was to use grant money to help cover this expense. After much discussion, Ms. Lee and the principal decided to solicit help from local businesses to pay for the roaming substitute.

Once time and resources for Fusion were in place, the next step was to select a roaming substitute. After discussing several possible candidates with the faculty, teachers chose Mrs. Chekhov, a retired engineer with artistic talents. It didn't take long for her to become a valued asset to the school. Mrs. Chekhov not only freed up time for peer observation but also offered enrichment lessons and tutored students. Any time there was an hour or two when she wasn't busy with Fusion, teachers signed up to have Mrs. Chekhov come to their class to share engineering and art lessons or to work one-on-one with students. Without a roaming substitute, these opportunities would not have been available.

At the conclusion of the first year of Fusion, Ms. Lee reflected on the implementation process. At first, it seemed impossible to find the time and resources necessary, especially for her socio-economically disadvantaged school. However, gaining the support of administrators and the school board, and breaking the financing of Fusion into four areas (teacher stipends, teacher facilitator, materials, and roaming substitute), made the difference. Together, Ms. Lee and the administrative team had used their imaginations to find ways to make Fusion possible. Ms. Lee wished she had had this experience prior to her one-year leave because now she feels she could have helped other schools maximize their use of time and resources.

Curriculum and Assessment

How can you increase teachers' expectations for themselves and for their students without allowing state tests to dominate the curriculum?

The strong emphasis placed on state assessment has helped schools gain a better understanding of students' levels of proficiency, but has this practice significantly enhanced learning? Test results are usually received late in the school year and are reported in a general fashion, making it difficult for teachers to remediate instruction (Marzano, 2003). Schools can resolve some of the problems associated with state testing through the use of formative assessment. Formative assessment does enhance learning, to considerable degrees, according to some research:

> An effect size of 0.7, if it could be achieved on a nationwide scale, would be equivalent to raising the mathematics achievement score of an "average" country like England, New Zealand or the United States into the "top five" after the Pacific rim countries of Singapore, Korea, Japan and Hong Kong. (Black & Wiliam, 1998, p. 61)

Scenario

To become better acquainted with personnel and to get a feel for ways to help schools improve, Mr. Bennett, the district superintendent, spends each Wednesday interacting with principals, teachers, and students at different schools. Although the district has invested thousands of dollars on textbooks in an effort to promote a core curriculum, a person would never know it based on what Superintendent Bennett sees when he makes his visits. Some schools have relaxed, social atmospheres where teachers pick and choose what to teach. A few teachers emphasize the adopted curriculum; others use textbooks abandoned by the district years ago or rely on the Internet for their curriculum. In some classrooms, students engage in a variety of hands-on learning activities, while in others they sit quietly, completing worksheets. Regardless of the instructional approach, Superintendent Bennett has difficulty seeing the correlation between learning activities and state standards.

Other schools are rigid and overly structured. Teachers are required to follow scripted programs focused on mastery of basic reading, writing, and math skills. Virtually every teacher teaches the same content, at the same time, and in the same way. Mr. Bennett is worried that the monotony of these schools is destroying students' desire to learn.

Superintendent Bennett would like to make some changes in his district. To begin with, he wants to increase the consistency of academic rigor. He believes students should have an equal opportunity to master essential knowledge and skills, as outlined in state and district standards, regardless of who their teacher is. In addition, some teachers seem to care more about their content area than about students. When students have difficulty grasping new concepts, these teachers blame students for academic failure rather than questioning the effectiveness of their teaching methodologies. Although student accountability is imperative, Superintendent Bennett wants teachers to accept more personal responsibility for student success. Finally, he wants to encourage schools to provide more enrichment to students. He is shocked with the emphasis on preparing students for state assessments at the expense of enriching curricula. Even though test scores are important, he believes science, history, art, and music are valuable, too.

Theory

One of the most important steps schools can take to ensure the success of every student is to develop a guaranteed and viable curriculum (Marzano, 2003). *Guaranteed* in this context means all students have the opportunity to learn essential knowledge and skills valued by the school or district. "States and districts give clear guidance to teachers regarding the content to be addressed in specific courses and at specific grade levels. It also means that individual teachers do not have the option to disregard or replace assigned content" (Marzano, 2003, p. 24). *Viable* means teachers have the instructional time available to adequately cover the content they are expected to address (Marzano, 2003).

Schools must also provide feedback as they monitor student progress toward mastering essential knowledge and skills. To have an impact on student achievement, feedback must be timely and specific to the content being learned, and students must receive feedback frequently throughout the learning process (Bangert-Drowns, Kulik, Kulik, & Morgan, 1991).

Assessment can help schools develop a guaranteed and viable curriculum as well as provide timely feedback to teachers and students. State tests can be used to set a common standard, determine whether students meet this standard, and serve accountability purposes. The goal of state testing should be to change the status quo, not rationalize it. Setting high expectations and then offering the support needed to meet these expectations can motivate teachers to improve instruction. However, high-stakes testing can also influence teachers to engage in practices that are not always in the best interest of students. For this reason, schools need the risk-free qualities of formative assessment. Balancing the use of summative assessment (tests that are given at the end of a learning experience, used to determine competence, and can sometimes be threatening) with formative assessment (tests that are designed to provide timely feedback throughout a learning experience, measure academic growth, and are not viewed as a threat) can ensure students master essential knowledge and skills without micromanaging teachers.

Implementing Fusion

Step 1: Make a clear distinction between high-stakes testing and formative assessment.

One way to increase teachers' expectations is to create a safe haven where they feel comfortable taking risks. Clearly distinguishing between high-stakes tests and formative assessment can help create this environment.

When teachers' jobs and reputation are based on test results, they naturally look for ways to preserve job security. In efforts to improve test scores, teachers may rely on rote memorization, overuse drills, or resort to mannerisms that could jeopardize the integrity of assessment. To prevent this from happening, formative assessment results must not be associated with job security or status.

Unclear standards and expectations make assessment threatening. It is difficult to prepare students to succeed on state tests when standards are vague and when the rigor, format, and content of state tests continually change. Providing teachers with formative assessments at the beginning of the year to be used as instructional guides and with samples of student work that illustrate various levels of proficiency clarify standards and expectations. Such clarity increases the likelihood that assessment will improve student achievement.

Unrealistic expectations can also make assessment threatening. Teacher effectiveness is normally based on the percentage of students who earn a proficient score on state tests. However, many students come to teachers performing well below grade level, with limited language proficiency or learning difficulties that prevent them from catching up to their peers in a year's time. Consequently, state test results can make teachers appear to be ineffective, regardless of the amount of growth students experience under their tutelage. For this reason, formative assessment should be content specific and based on student growth.

Finally, publicizing test results or using them to compare teachers can be threatening. The goal of Fusion is to motivate teachers to compete against themselves rather than their colleagues. Therefore, formative test results should never be publicized or used to compare teachers.

Step 2: Provide guidelines that encourage teachers to incorporate formative assessment into daily practice.

The Menu of Alternatives described in Chapter 1 offers a category designed to encourage teachers to increase the productivity of assessment. Teachers complete Level 1 and earn a stipend of $200 for completing the criteria listed in Figure 5.1. Teachers who use formative assessment for two consecutive years meet the requirements for Level 2 and earn 8 points toward a permanent

---

Figure 5.1   Criteria for Developing Formative Assessment

The teacher provides documentation of the use of

❏ a pre- and post-test that is aligned with state standards, comprehensive in nature, and matches or exceeds the rigor of state testing.

❏ a minimum of five periodic assessments that match or exceed the rigor of state testing, measure student progress toward mastery of state and district standards, and prepare students for the post-test.

❏ teacher goals that measure the effectiveness of instruction. These goals are based on students' pre-test performance and must be set for the class as a whole and for student subgroups. The teacher must also use charts or graphs to illustrate student progress toward reaching these goals.

❏ student goals that are individualized, focused on growth, and based on students' pre-test performance.

❏ student binders or portfolios that contain pre- and post-tests, periodic assessments, and charts or graphs that illustrate student goals and progress toward reaching these goals.

❏ strategies that reinforce effort and provide recognition to students when they reach achievement goals.

increase in pay. The remainder of this chapter describes methodologies some teachers at Osmond Elementary have used to meet this criterion.

Step 3: Use formative assessment to establish high performance standards.

A common belief for years was that it was physically impossible for humans to run a mile in less than four minutes. Roger Bannister, a neurologist from the United Kingdom, thought differently. After numerous attempts, he finally broke the 4-minute barrier on May 6, 1954, with a time of 3:59.4 (Bannister, 2004). Since then, numerous runners have completed the mile in less than 4 minutes, and the current world record is 3:43.13 (International Association of Athletics Federations, 2009). Just as the 4-minute standard lifted the mile race to new levels of excellence, setting high academic standards through formative assessment can lift education to new levels of performance. Once teachers feel confident that assessment developed through Fusion is not punitive, they can work together to create challenging pre- and post-tests and periodic assessments that boost academic rigor.

Pre- and post-tests are common rigorous assessments designed to measure students' understanding of *all* essential knowledge and skills within a content area. Students take pre-tests shortly after the beginning of a school year (or semester in secondary schools) and then take the same test at the end of the year or semester to measure academic growth. Pre- and post-tests are content specific: they assess specifically what is taught. This allows teachers to evaluate the effectiveness of their instruction. For this reason, every teacher, regardless of their content area or grade level, can use formative assessment to determine which students have mastered the goals and objectives of the course they teach. Because pre- and post-tests are comprehensive, teachers must concentrate on using best practices to help students learn and retain important knowledge and skills that will be assessed months after information is presented.

Periodic assessments are benchmarks or checkpoints used to inform teachers and students about academic progress as they prepare for the post-test. Periodic assessments are similar to pre- and post-tests in that they match or exceed the rigor of state testing, are common among grade levels or content areas, and match a school's curriculum. They are different from pre- and post-tests because they are shorter; they are administered throughout the learning experience; and if students perform poorly on a unit test, teachers use this as an opportunity to reteach information or make other necessary interventions. Because periodic tests are formative in nature, teachers decide whether these scores influence students' grades.

There are two types of periodic assessments. The first focuses on small amounts of information such as a unit test. For example, at the end of a geometry unit, teachers use a periodic assessment to determine students' understanding of geometry. Or, if a teacher has recently taught students how to write persuasive essays, the test would measure students' ability to perform this task and nothing else.

The second type of periodic assessment is similar to a trimester test. It is comprehensive in nature but only focuses on information presented to students thus far in the school year. For example, a first-trimester math test may assess students' understanding of number concepts, addition, subtraction, and estimation. The second-trimester test assesses not only these topics but also multiplication, division, fractions, and decimals. These assessments gradually become more comprehensive until students develop the skills and stamina necessary to succeed on the post-test.

Step 4: Use pre-tests to gather baseline data.

Teachers administer the pre-test at the beginning of the school year or semester to collect baseline data. Students are then divided into subgroups based on their performance. Because the pre-test assesses information students haven't been taught, scores will naturally be low. Here are the guidelines we use at Osmond Elementary to classify students:

- Subgroup 1: 0–15 percent
- Subgroup 2: 16–25 percent
- Subgroup 3: 26–39 percent
- Subgroup 4: 40–100 percent

Figure 5.2 shows a hypothetical classroom of 4th grade students' scores on a math pre-test based on these guidelines.

Figure 5.2 4th Grade Math Pretest Results

Student Subgroup	Percent on Pre-test	Goal	Post-test
Group 1: (0–15%)			
Kisha	5	45	
Ben	8	48	
Jordan	13	53	
	Average: 9%	Average: 49%	
Group 2: (16%–25%)			
Emma	16	56	
Billy	18	58	
Andrew	20	60	
Natausha	25	65	
	Average: 20%	Average: 60%	
Group 3: (26%–39%)			
Mikayla	27	67	
Christopher	28	68	
Michael	30	70	
Rachel	35	75	
Krystal	38	78	
	Average: 32%	Average: 72%	
Group 4: (40%–100%)			
Tanner	42	82	
Megan	50	90	
	Average: 46%	Average: 86%	
Class Average:	25%	65%	

Step 5: Encourage teachers to set personal goals that help them monitor the effectiveness of instruction.

Teacher effectiveness has a direct effect on student achievement. Students who spend a year with a highly effective teacher normally show academic gains of approximately 53 percentage points, whereas students who spend a year with an average or highly ineffective teacher improve their academic performance by about 34 and 14 percentage points, respectively (see Glass, McGaw, & Smith, 1981; Haycock, 1998; Wright, Horn, & Sanders, 1997).

These guidelines can be used to facilitate the goal-setting process. In essence, these are "teacher achievement" rather than "student achievement" goals. For example, if an individual wanted to be an ineffective teacher, she could set goals at 14 percent higher than students' pre-test performance. If a person wanted to be an average teacher, she could set goals about 34 percent higher. Or, if she wanted to prove to herself that she is highly effective, she would strive to help students meet goals that are 35 to 53 percent higher than their pre-test performance. To illustrate, let's say Emma is a student who scored 16 percent on a math pre-test. Her teacher, Mrs. Bocardo, wants to challenge herself by helping Emma improve her performance on the post-test by 40 percent. Therefore, Mrs. Bocardo's goal is to apply best practices in a manner that will help Emma score at least 56 percent on the math post-test.

Once a teacher has set goals for individual students, she calculates an average for each subgroup as well as a class average. Look at Figure 5.2 again, which shows pre-test results on a 4th grade math assessment and a teacher's goal to help students increase their performance on the post-test by 40 percent. For example, Emma, Billy, Andrew, and Natausha scored between 16 and 25 percent on the math pre-test. As a result, they have been placed in Group 2. As a subgroup, these students averaged 20 percent on the pre-test. Because Mrs. Bocardo's goal is to improve student achievement by 40 percent, she strives to help Group 2 average 60 percent on the post-test.

There will always be situations when students' pre-test performance does not represent their true ability. As a result, initial goals may be too difficult or too easy, which can discourage students rather than motivate them. Teachers should use their professional judgment to determine when they need to make adjustments to students' goals. Teachers must also be careful not to set advanced students' goals too high. For example, if a student scored 58 percent on the pre-test, maintaining an average of 98 percent on periodic assessments might be unrealistic. It doesn't matter how smart or gifted a person is, people are prone to make mistakes. For this reason, I recommend not setting goals higher than 92 percent to allow for a margin of error. It is better for advanced students to experience success by scoring higher than their goal than it is for them to consistently fail to reach their goal.

Step 6: Teachers create graphs illustrating the progress of student subgroups.

Once teachers have used the pre-test to gather baseline data and have set personal goals, the next step is to monitor progress toward reaching these goals. After presenting information to students, teachers administer periodic assessments. Then they graph the class average and the average of student subgroups as shown in Figure 5.3. This graph is placed in a binder, enabling teachers to monitor their effectiveness with student subgroups.

Graphing results provides a visual representation that offers specific feedback to teachers. For example, rather than saying the teacher in this scenario is good at teaching math, Figure 5.3 illustrates that she teaches geometry and fractions exceptionally well, but her methodologies for teaching number concepts are not reaching students in Group 1 as they should. This information is helpful when teachers meet together to discuss ways to enhance learning because it shows them specifically what they need to improve.

Graphing results also allows teachers to experience short-term success (Schmoker, 1999). Teachers feel a great sense of satisfaction when student subgroups reach their goal, which energizes the improvement process. As long as goal setting remains non-

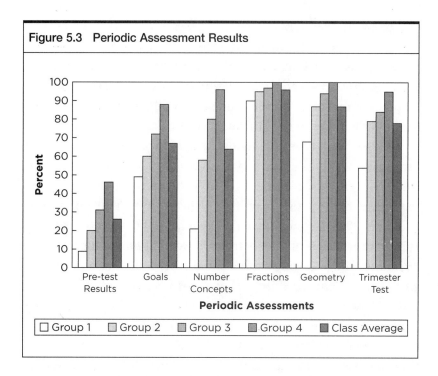

Figure 5.3   Periodic Assessment Results

threatening, teachers feel a natural inclination to increase their expectations. For example, let's say the teacher in this scenario reaches her goal to help students improve their performance by 40 percent. The next year she may increase her goal to 45 percent, making Fusion a positive way to raise teacher expectations.

It is imperative for leaders to respect teachers' privacy. Requiring teachers to share graphs with administrators changes the nature of these assessments from formative to summative. An important purpose of state testing is to allow leaders to evaluate teacher competence. There is no need to use formative assessment for this purpose as well.

Step 7: Motivate students to take ownership for their learning.

Once teachers have set personal goals, they create graphs for individual students. There are two types of student graphs. The first is useful with isolated units of information. For example, math is composed of addition, subtraction, geometry, and so on. At the end of a unit, teachers can simply assess students' understanding of the concepts taught and thus use the same goal for each unit. To illustrate, Emma scored 16 percent on the math pre-test, and Mrs. Bocardo set a goal for her to improve her performance to 56 percent on the post-test. The goal of 56 percent can be used for periodic assessments throughout the school year.

The second type of student graph promotes growth over time. For example, when a student writes a personal narrative, there isn't necessarily one right or wrong answer, but there are variations in the quality of writing. Using the 6 + 1 Traits of Writing (Culham, 2003) as a guide, let's say a school develops a scoring rubric where each of the six traits is worth 4 points for a total of 24 points. The following scores could represent students' level of writing proficiency: 0–8, Below Basic; 9–14, Basic; 15–21, Proficient; 22–24, Advanced.

A personal narrative may score 3 in Word Choice, 1 in Sentence Fluency, and 2 in the other four areas of writing for a total score of 12. Based on these guidelines, this student's writing proficiency would be considered Basic. Moving from Basic to Proficient on the next writing prompt may be unrealistic for this student. However, helping him improve his Sentence Fluency score from a 1 to a 2 or 3 is a sensible goal. As students' writing ability evolves over time, so should goals.

Once student goals have been determined, students are given a copy of their graphs, which are placed in student binders. Students track their progress by graphing periodic assessment results next to the bar illustrating the goal for each test. Emma's math progress and Jordan's writing progress are depicted in Figures 5.4 and 5.5.

Now that students have goals as well as a tangible way to track their progress, the next challenge is to motivate them to do their best. The strategy Reinforcing Effort and Providing Recognition (Marzano et al., 2001b) is a powerful motivational tool that can help accomplish this task. Students learn that the effort they put into paying attention during class, completing assignments in a timely and acceptable manner, doing their homework, studying,

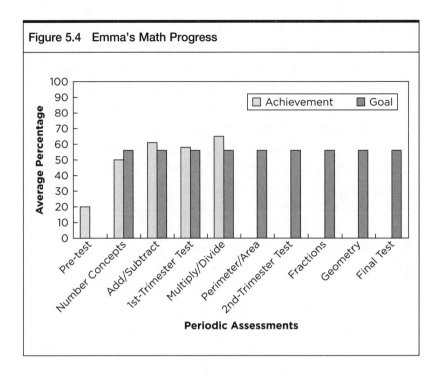

Figure 5.4 Emma's Math Progress

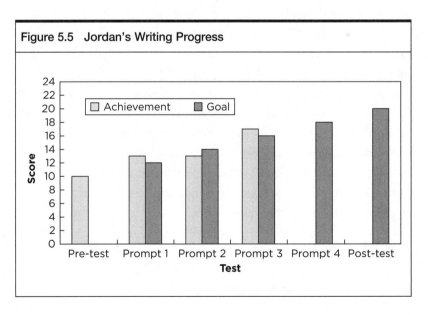

Figure 5.5 Jordan's Writing Progress

and asking questions when they don't understand a concept makes a difference in their performance on periodic assessments. They also learn that recognition comes after meeting a challenging yet realistic predetermined standard. For example, when Emma scores at least 56 percent on a unit math test or when Jordan reaches a writing goal, these students meet the predetermined standard and are recognized. Recognition does not have to be extravagant. Sometimes educators forget that students gain satisfaction simply from reaching a challenging goal. Therefore, student rewards should never outweigh the personal satisfaction that comes from experiencing success. If some students do not meet their goal, instead of receiving recognition, they are encouraged to do their best to meet the predetermined standard next time.

In conclusion, formative assessment can enhance the goal-setting process. The strategies described in this chapter allow students *and* teachers to experience short- and long-term success as they strive to reach challenging goals. This approach also allows all students to experience success, regardless of whether they have a learning disability. Emma, for example, is likely a student requiring special services. If she averaged 56 percent on math tests in a traditional classroom, she would feel like a failure. Over time, she would eventually become discouraged and perhaps even engage in at-risk behaviors. Conversely, if Emma were in a Fusion classroom, she would have reason to celebrate an average score of 56 percent because an increase of 40 percent on grade-level assessments is an above-average performance on her part. If Emma continues to receive effective instruction as she progresses through the educational system and continues to do her best, she will eventually close the achievement gap between herself and her peers. Thus, when used appropriately, as in this example, assessment can become one of education's greatest allies.

Step 8: Use formative assessment to gather a body of evidence.

Schools can use the assessments and graphs described in this chapter to create a body of evidence. Pre-tests, periodic assessments, student graphs and post-tests are placed in three-ring binders or three-tab folders (depending on the number of students and the amount of storage space) and are stored in the classroom. Students are responsible for placing periodic assessments into their binders and for updating graphs so that they can track progress throughout the year. To maintain confidentiality, personal information such as standardized test results or items normally found in cumulative folders are *not* part of student binders. If students require special services and as a result spend the bulk of their time outside the regular classroom, resource teachers save formative assessments illustrating student mastery of essential knowledge and skills. This evidence allows all teachers, regardless of what they teach, to monitor student progress as well as their effectiveness as a teacher.

Student binders motivate students to do their best. When the time comes to take the post-test, students enjoy looking back at work samples knowing that they have developed the skills necessary to solve problems they didn't understand at the beginning of the year. In addition, student binders help teachers organize important information, making it easier to confer with students and parents. Rather than relying solely on grades, which can sometimes be vague and misleading, student binders contain detailed information regarding progress toward mastery of state standards. Information in the binder allows parents to take a proactive role in their child's education and facilitates the intervention process. Equally important, student binders provide consistency. Students are challenged with the same standards and expectations, regardless of whose class they are in. Thus, formative assessment can facilitate the development of a guaranteed and viable curriculum without micromanaging instruction.

Connecting Fusion with Best Practices

Fusion facilitates the development of a guaranteed and viable curriculum. Encouraging teachers to use state and district standards to distinguish between knowledge and skills that are essential for students to learn and those that are supplemental greatly reduces the amount of content teachers are expected to teach (Marzano, 2003). The use of common formative assessments, scoring rubrics, and student exemplars clarifies state standards and increases academic consistency.

Fusion applies research pertaining to short- and long-term goals and provides timely feedback throughout the learning process that is specific to the content being taught (Bangert-Drowns et al., 1991). Gathering a body of evidence allows teachers to determine specifically what assistance students need. Graphing results provides a visual representation of academic progress that enhances communication among teachers, parents, and students.

From Our School to Yours

Development of a Guaranteed and Viable Curriculum

Educators at Osmond Elementary began the quest to develop a guaranteed and viable curriculum with the content area of math. Reviewing a list of objectives for the 4th, 5th, and 6th grades, we were amused to find that there were more objectives to teach than instructional days available. For example, 6th grade teachers were expected to teach 220 math objectives (many of which included multiple concepts) in 170 days. We used state standards to help us distinguish between objectives that were essential for students to learn and those that were supplemental (Marzano, 2003). Every teacher had a different opinion and was afraid to eliminate something that might be important. We solved this problem by reassuring teachers that all we were doing was prioritizing what we taught; we could always teach supplemental information if instructional time allowed. With this understanding, we narrowed our list to fewer than 90 essential objectives per grade level. This simple step made a significant improvement in student achievement because teachers no longer felt pressured to rush through the math curriculum.

After aligning math, we focused on reading. This subject was more difficult because of the diverse ways to teach reading. For example, some teachers relied on novels, while others preferred basal readers. Some stressed fiction; others, nonfiction. We also found that as students progressed to higher grade levels, less emphasis was placed on skills instruction.

We used the publication *Put Reading First* (USDE, 2001) as a guide to help determine exactly what reading skills needed to be reinforced to improve comprehension. These were added to the Menu of Alternatives, and teachers and paraprofessionals were encouraged to use Fusion to incorporate these skills into daily instruction. To help balance our literacy program, we discussed the amount of instructional time that should be used for emphasizing fiction, nonfiction, and skills instruction. Following that, we compiled formative assessments that measured students' ability to comprehend a variety of reading genres (e.g., realistic fiction, fantasy, expository text, functional reading, and poetry) and to apply various reading skills (identifying the main idea, distinguishing between fact and opinion, detecting the sequence, identifying story elements, etc.). We are now in the process of selecting a core list of vocabulary words that help build students' academic background knowledge, using Fusion to learn effective ways to provide vocabulary instruction.

Our last goal was to align our writing curriculum. Every teacher, armed with copies of state and district standards, had a different perspective on what constituted writing instruction. Some teachers focused on grammar and used worksheets for their curriculum. Others relied on Daily Oral Language (Great Source Education Group, 1993) or journal writing. A few teachers used Writing Workshop to teach narrative and expository writing.

To provide more consistency, we adopted a districtwide program that emphasized both narrative and expository writing using the Writing Workshop format. Then we modified state and district scoring rubrics until we had a rubric that matched our curriculum and could be used as an instructional tool by students. Next, we chose several writing prompts for each grade level. Students responded to these prompts, and teachers met together to select anchor papers that represented different levels of proficiency. Student exemplars were placed into binders and given to teachers, who used them to evaluate writing and to enhance instruction. For example, on completing a writing prompt, students were divided into cooperative groups and were given anchor papers ranging from basic to advanced. Students classified their peers' writing (which was kept anonymous) by placing writing samples on top of the anchor papers they most closely resembled. Then students explained their reasoning. At the end of the activity, students set personal goals to improve their writing.

Developing common assessments was perhaps the most important step we took in establishing a guaranteed and viable curriculum. We intentionally set the bar high so that if students could pass our formative assessments, they would easily earn a proficient score on state tests. Because teachers were involved with this process, they felt ownership; consequently, even teachers who previously weren't involved with Fusion valued formative assessment. We also found that when teachers were striving to meet the same standards represented by schoolwide tests, academic rigor and consistency naturally improved.

Paper-and-Pencil and Computerized Tests as Formative Assessments

We found that using a combination of paper-and-pencil and computerized assessments was helpful. Paper-and-pencil tests provided a tangible standard that represented the academic rigor of our school. They increased the value of student binders because actual samples of student work were more meaningful than a compilation of percentages or grades. Also, allowing parents to see how their child completed specific test items improved the quality of parent-teacher conferences. Finally, paper-and-pencil assessments and the use of goal setting as outlined in this chapter played an important role in student motivation.

Computerized tests were also helpful. For several years, our state offered formative computerized assessments that were created by the same company that developed our state test.

The format of these assessments resembled state tests, they were convenient to administer, scoring was automatic, and students gained valuable experience taking online tests. When students completed a test, teachers could print a report showing students' percentages and which problems students had missed. This print-out was added to student binders, and the results were graphed as if students had taken a paper-and-pencil test.

Assessment of Students with Special Needs

At Osmond Elementary, even students with special needs take grade-level formative assessments. Classroom and resource teachers are then encouraged to differentiate instruction in a manner that maximizes student growth on the post-test. We have found that requiring students to take formative assessments, even if they qualify for special services, exposes them to grade-level expectations and reduces their anxiety when taking state tests.

Our Experience with Setting Goals

At first, we weren't sure how to go about setting student goals. Traditionally, teachers used the same goal for every student. For example, students were expected to score 80 percent on the post-test, regardless of their pre-test performance. But this goal didn't seem fair, because an advanced student who scored 45 percent on the pre-test would have to improve her performance by 35 percent on the post-test, whereas a struggling student who scored 10 percent on the pre-test would have to improve his performance by 70 percent. As a result, students who needed the most encouragement were also the most likely to fail.

We also tried tripling pre-test scores for low-performing students and doubling the pre-test scores of high-performing students. For instance, if a student scored 10 percent on the pre-test, his goal was to reach 30 percent on the post-test. If a student scored 45 percent on the pre-test, his goal was to score 90 percent on the post-test. However, these guidelines increased the achievement gap between low- and high-performing students. The struggling student in this example would be expected to improve his performance by 20 percent on the post-test, whereas the advanced student needed to improve by 45 percent to reach his goal.

Finally, we applied the information shared in Steps 5 and 6 of this chapter. It made sense to expect the same amount of growth from every student. For example, expecting 40 percent growth from a student who scored 10 percent on the pre-test as well as from a student who scored 45 percent was fair. At first, teachers didn't think it was possible for low-performing students to experience the same amount of growth as their peers. However, we found that increasing teacher expectations had a positive influence on all students, especially those with special needs.

Test Results and Teacher Relationships

We learned through experience that teachers are sensitive to sharing test results. If scores are high, colleagues sometimes think the teacher is trying to show off. If test scores are low, peers tend to question the teacher's competence. After several heated discussions, we discovered that it was more beneficial to ask for advice in a general way than it was to share actual results. For instance, if a teacher was struggling with teaching division, he could say, "I have tried these strategies . . . and have observed these results. . . . Does anyone have suggestions I could try?" More specifically, this math teacher might say, "I have tried to teach the steps for division using a story about 'the division family.' In a division family, there is a dad, mom, sister, and brother. Dad means divide, Mom means multiply, Sister means subtract, and Brother means bring down. When dividing numbers, you basically repeat these steps until you solve the problem. However, this strategy doesn't seem to work for several students. Does anyone have other suggestions I could try?"

We also learned that passing pre- and post-tests from one grade level to the next strained interpersonal relationships. At the end of the first year we used formative assessment, we removed everything from student binders except for reading, writing, and math post-tests and then gave these binders to the next grade level. Although actual samples of student work were more helpful than state test scores, sharing this information revealed teachers' strengths and weaknesses. Some teachers became judgmental of their colleagues, which had a negative impact on collegiality.

Scenario

Words cannot describe the elation Superintendent Bennett felt when he learned that his school district had passed the accreditation process with flying colors. State officials were impressed with the consistency of academic rigor and with the body of evidence contained in student binders. When asked how his district had accomplished such an amazing task, Superintendent Bennett attributed success to three factors: (1) years of participation in study groups and peer observation had fostered an environment of collegiality; (2) administrators had convinced teachers that formative assessment would never become high-stakes tests, which increased their willingness to create rigorous assessments; and (3) sufficient time during contract hours had been provided to complete this project.

Superintendent Bennett elaborated by sharing the process his district had used to develop a guaranteed and viable curriculum. To begin with, this concept was introduced in a manner that helped principals and teachers understand why a guaranteed and viable curriculum was necessary. Next, faculties were organized into grade-level or content area teams that compiled a list of state and district standards, eliminating those that duplicated information. This list was then used to determine which knowledge and skills were essential for all students to learn and which were supplemental. After instructional priorities were identified, teachers met in multigrade-level teams to work on vertical alignment. Educators concluded the process by developing formative pre- and post-tests and periodic assessments. Rather than reinventing the wheel, teachers relied on existing resources to help them compile test items. The bar was intentionally set high so that if students could perform satisfactorily on formative tests, they would easily succeed on state tests.

At the conclusion of the first year, grade-level and content area teachers met once again to make minor revisions to formative assessments. They also compared student work to determine which samples represented true proficiency. Master copies of pre- and post-tests, periodic assessments, and samples of student proficiency were then placed into binders and given to all teachers within the district.

Although developing a guaranteed and viable curriculum was a challenging process, it didn't take long to reap the benefits of this hard work. The assessment packet was helpful, especially to new teachers, because it clarified the district's expectations and provided anchor papers that clearly exhibited results students were expected to achieve. Reducing the amount of content teachers had to cover allowed more time for quality instruction. This made learning easier and helped students retain what they had been taught. As teachers improved their ability to teach essential knowledge and skills, they focused more attention on enrichment, which made school enjoyable without jeopardizing the core curriculum. As a result, Superintendent Bennett feels confident that every student in his school district receives a high-quality education.

Systematic Intervention

How do you encourage classroom teachers to provide timely
interventions without neglecting a subgroup of students?

Most schools identify and provide services to students experiencing significant learning difficulties. However, many schools do not have a systematic approach to assisting students who do not have learning disabilities but struggle now and then with academic concepts. For example, let's say a student has difficulty mastering the multiplication facts but has a fairly good grasp of other math concepts. Unless a label such as "Title I" or "special ed" is attached to this student, she will probably not receive help other than that offered by the classroom teacher. What if the classroom teacher doesn't provide remediation? Also, in an attempt to leave no child behind, schools tend to overlook advanced students. How might neglecting these students influence the future of our country? Ironically, schools would find better ways to reach all students if they focused more attention on enrichment. Therefore, a sound, systematic approach to interventions meets the needs of all students, not just those with learning disabilities.

Scenario
Mrs. Kasahara is a nontenured 3rd grade teacher at a traditional K–6 elementary school. Her class is composed of students who can breeze through the Harry Potter series and others who

struggle to read a 1st grade basal. The same is true in math and writing: many students catch on quickly, while others do not. Mrs. Kasahara wants to meet the needs of all of her students, but when there is such a span in ability, she knows her tendency is to focus on the struggling students and give time fillers to her more gifted students. This approach is frustrating, but she knows her end-of-year evaluation as a productive teacher is based mostly on student performance on state tests.

Mrs. Kasahara believes in mainstreaming special education students as much as possible. The problem is, inclusion at her school means classroom teachers take full responsibility for students with special needs while resource teachers complete paperwork. As a result, she finds herself using the same instructional techniques with all of her students, regardless of whether they have a learning disability. She is also frustrated with the referral process because it relies heavily on teacher intuition. Because Mrs. Kasahara doesn't have a background in special education, she has difficulty determining when to initiate the intervention process.

In addition, Mrs. Kasahara is concerned about the advanced students at her school. Many of these students could earn a proficient score on state tests at the beginning of the school year, yet they are required to complete the same work as their peers. Boredom often leads to off-task behaviors and underachievement. Mrs. Kasahara tries to stretch high-ability students' thinking by assigning them challenging questions found in classroom textbooks. However, the students view this as a punishment rather than a reward because they do more work than their peers.

Mrs. Kasahara sincerely wants to do what's best for every student in her class. Unfortunately, her undergraduate studies didn't provide details for timely interventions to assist students with learning difficulties or creative ideas to challenge high-ability students. Mrs. Kasahara would feel more successful as a teacher if her school provided more guidelines and staff development in these areas.

Characteristics of a Systematic Approach to Interventions

Schools need a systematic approach to interventions that ensures students receive the assistance they need regardless of the class they are in. Rather than relying on intuition to initiate this process, teachers need a clear understanding of when student interventions are necessary and the procedures they must follow once students demonstrate learning difficulties, and they must be held responsible for following these procedures. Consistency is thus an important characteristic of a systematic approach to interventions.

Interventions are more likely to benefit students when they are administered in a timely manner. For instance, master teachers naturally monitor students as they practice concepts introduced in a lesson. When they encounter students who don't understand what was taught, expert teachers immediately intervene by presenting the information differently. Also, when formative or summative test results indicate that students don't understand a particular concept, master teachers intervene within a day or two to prevent a lapse of time from compounding learning difficulties. Finally, when it becomes apparent that students may require special services, master teachers instigate the referral process immediately.

Education's highest priority should be to provide teachers with the skills and necessary resources to help students succeed in regular classrooms. Schools must be careful not to label students, intervene prematurely, or place challenging students into special education simply because classroom teachers do not want to work with them. Even when students qualify for special services, they have the right to remain with their peers in a regular classroom setting as long as students with special needs demonstrate the ability to learn in a regular classroom setting and attention problems, behaviors, and learning disabilities do not interfere with the education of other students.

A simple yet important characteristic of systematic interventions is for teachers to rely on one another to teach students.

This approach can happen through collaboration, nonthreatening forms of peer mentoring, team teaching, or a temporary exchange of students to reteach information.

Most classroom teachers feel extreme pressure to help students perform well on end-of-year state tests. However, sometimes students spend the bulk of their time with resource teachers and specialists, not the classroom teacher. All professionals responsible for educating a child should be held accountable for student progress, not just classroom teachers.

The effectiveness of the intervention process is closely connected to the capability of the individuals administering the interventions. Once teachers reach the limit of their expertise, they can do little more than repeat what has *not* worked previously. For this reason, professional development is a crucial component of the intervention process. Teachers must master hundreds of best practices if they truly want to differentiate instruction for students. Therefore, schools must be proactive by offering superb professional development opportunities.

Implementing Fusion

Step 1: Use common criteria to determine when student interventions are necessary.

The first step to developing a systematic approach to student interventions is to adopt common criteria for use by all teachers in determining when interventions are necessary. Chapter 5 describes how schools could use formative pre- and post-tests and periodic assessments to gather baseline data and monitor student progress. Because these tests are content specific, common among grade levels, and administered frequently, they can provide the consistency schools need to determine when student interventions are necessary.

Step 2: Determine indicators that trigger the intervention process.

Once teachers are using the same criteria to monitor student progress, the next step is to determine indicators that trigger the intervention process. Chapter 5 describes how teachers could compare students' pretest performance with periodic assessment results to measure academic growth. An increase of 14 percent would be considered small; 34 percent, average; and over 50 percent, exceptional (Glass et al., 1981; Haycock, 1998). Schools may decide that when students score 65 percent or lower on a periodic assessment or when students demonstrate less than 30 percent growth, an intervention may be necessary. At the other end of the performance spectrum, students who consistently score higher than 96 percent on formative assessments may need to be challenged.

Step 3: Clearly articulate steps classroom teachers must take when students experience learning difficulties.

As teachers become aware of learning difficulties, they must determine the cause and then make the instructional adjustments necessary to help students succeed. This is a cyclical process in which teachers provide instruction, assess student learning, diagnose why students are experiencing learning difficulties, and then make the necessary interventions.

Instruct

All teachers have four fundamental instructional responsibilities. The first is to provide students with multiple exposures to content by using a variety of instructional strategies. Second, teachers must ensure that students receive the practice necessary to master essential knowledge and skills. Third, teachers are responsible for organizing and sequencing curriculum in a manner that maximizes students' opportunity to learn. Finally, teachers must maintain a classroom environment conducive to learning (Marzano, 2003; Marzano et al., 2001b).

Assess

As teachers deliver instruction to students, they should use formative and summative assessment to determine to what degree students understand the content being taught. When students score lower than 65 percent on periodic assessments or demonstrate less than 30 percent growth, teachers should move to the next step of the intervention process, which is to discover why students are performing in such a manner.

Diagnose

Similar to how doctors study evidence before determining the nature of an illness, educators need to evaluate data gathered through assessment to help them determine why students are experiencing difficulties. Attention, attitude, and ability are three general reasons why students struggle in school.

Perhaps the most important question teachers can ask is whether students are paying attention to instruction. Obviously, if students are distracted while the teacher presents new information, they will likely experience learning difficulties. When inattentiveness is an issue, teachers should consider whether they are presenting information in a manner that students find engaging.

Once a teacher has determined whether struggling students are paying attention, the next step is to determine whether students have an attitude, or mental state, conducive to learning. Attitude can be broken down into several subcategories:

• *Teacher-student relationship:* Do the teacher and student have a positive interpersonal relationship? What can be done to improve rapport?

• *Perception of school:* Does the student enjoy learning? Does he find the content appealing? Is the student bored or frustrated?

• *Habits:* Does the student complete classroom assignments and homework in a timely manner? Is the quality of her work acceptable? Does the student come to class on time, prepared to learn?

• *Behavior:* Is the student overly active or passive? Does the student's classroom behavior interfere with his learning? Does the student's behavior interfere with the learning of others?

• *Self-esteem:* Does the student have a healthy self-esteem? Does she possess the social skills necessary to interact with others? Does the student have friends who are a positive influence?

- *Obstacles:* Is the student dealing with difficult issues at home, with friends, or with authority figures? Could he be experimenting with sex, drugs, alcohol, or other self-destructive behaviors? Is the student a victim of violence or other forms of abuse? Is there a language barrier that could be inhibiting the student? Could he have hearing or vision problems that have not been detected?

The final step is to analyze a student's ability. Does the student have the background knowledge and experiences necessary to learn what is being taught? Is the student capable of completing the work required of other students? Is there evidence of a learning disability that hinders the student? What is the learning disability?

Intervene

Once teachers have determined the cause of students' learning difficulties, the next step is to intervene. Teachers should start with small interventions and then gradually work toward bigger, more extreme interventions. The use of flowcharts can be helpful. Figure 6.1 illustrates a flowchart designed to offer general guidelines that can assist teachers with the intervention process. The "intervene" column has not been sectioned off because some of the same interventions could be used to influence attention, attitude, or ability.

Creating flowcharts should be a collaborative process where teachers meet together to determine what steps should be taken when students encounter learning difficulties. These charts must be tailored to meet the unique circumstances of individual schools. For example, inner-city schools have different needs than rural schools. Secondary schools face challenges that elementary schools don't have. Some schools have a large percentage of English language learners, and other schools do not. As teachers discover effective interventions, these strategies are added to the Menu of Alternatives described in Chapter 1, and Fusion can be used to help them learn these new strategies. For example, perhaps a teacher discovers stations (Tomlinson, 1999) to be an effective way to assist students that need additional instruction.

Figure 6.1 The Intervention Process

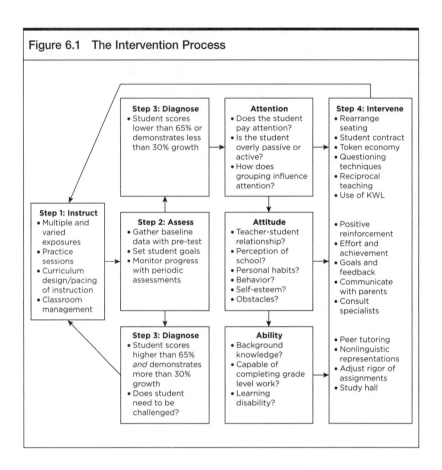

Or, another teacher may find that orbital studies (Tomlinson, 1999) help motivate reluctant learners. Criteria could be developed for these strategies and teachers could use the Fusion mastery process to learn them.

Obviously, there will always be situations when teachers do not possess the skills necessary to properly diagnose or intervene with students experiencing learning difficulties. Under these circumstances teachers must consult with professionals who do have such expertise.

Step 4: Involve colleagues with the intervention process.

Sometimes it is difficult for teachers to determine why students are experiencing learning difficulties. Training educators to use observation instruments designed to gather specific data could help solve this problem. Adhering to the principles of Fusion (see Chapter 2) allows teachers to provide objective feedback to one another without jeopardizing interpersonal relationships. Let's say 10 students are not performing as they should on periodic assessments, and the classroom teacher is having difficulty determining why. He could invite a peer to come to his classroom and conduct a "student on-task and off-task behavior analysis" (Glickman et al., 2004, p. 263). To conduct this sort of analysis, an observer stays in the classroom for a total of 25 minutes. The observer begins a new sweep of the classroom every 5 minutes. During each sweep, the observer focuses on the underperforming students for about 20 to 30 seconds—or, in this example, 10 students in 5 minutes. The observer then records what she sees based on the specific on-task and off-task behaviors listed at the bottom of the chart. After completing the observation, the observer places the form on her colleague's desk and exits the room without critiquing the instructional performance of her peer. (See Glickman et al., 2004, to learn more about a variety of observation instruments.)

Step 5: Establish a schoolwide system of interventions.

Schools need to have a detailed plan that offers a variety of ways to assist students. The purpose of this plan is to offer general guidelines to classroom teachers that help them know when they should begin the referral process. This system should be tiered so that if interventions at one level do not meet student needs, there is a backup plan. Figure 6.2 illustrates a schoolwide system of interventions. The remainder of this section explains the diagram.

The first level, or foundation of the system, places full responsibility on the classroom teacher. The second level provides additional assistance to students experiencing minor learning difficulties. The third level involves special education services using an inclusion model. The fourth level involves special education with a variety of pullout services. Alternate programs are

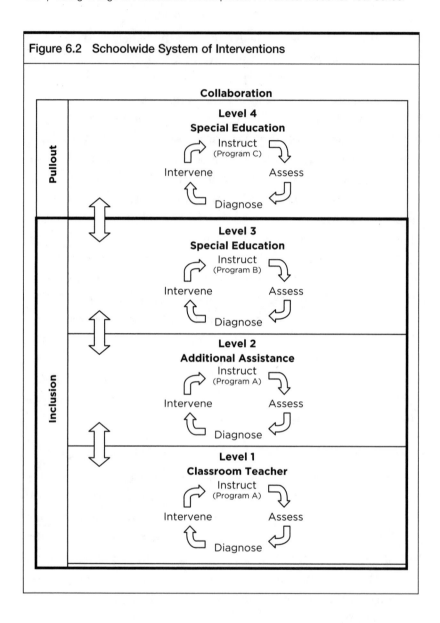

Figure 6.2 Schoolwide System of Interventions

used as the basis of instruction once students reach Levels 3 and 4. For example, a school may choose the Writing Workshop (Calkins & Martinelli, 2006) to be the core curriculum for providing writing instruction. This program would be used at Levels 1 and 2 of the intervention process. However, when students don't respond to this program, educators may decide to use the 6 + 1

Traits of Writing (Culham, 2003) as a Level 3 intervention, and Fundamentals in Sentence Writing (Schumaker & Sheldon, 1998) could be used as a Level 4 intervention.

Level 1: Classroom Teacher

The classroom teacher begins the intervention process by using best practices, applying adopted schoolwide programs, conducting formative assessment, setting goals, identifying students who are not performing as they should, determining why targeted students are struggling, and then making a variety of attempts to help these students through differentiated instruction. (Differentiated instruction will be addressed in the next chapter.) The flowchart in Figure 6.1 facilitates this process. It is the responsibility of the classroom teacher to get help from colleagues when faced with difficulties that go beyond the limits of his expertise.

Level 2: Additional Assistance

After the classroom teacher has exhausted his repertoire of strategies, struggling students move to the second level of the intervention process, where they receive additional assistance from other individuals. This support can be as simple as helping students stay on task or briefly reteaching information at the conclusion of a lesson. Title I services, the use of paraprofessionals, and after-school programs where teachers exchange students for remediation or enrichment are examples of ways schools can provide additional assistance to students.

Level 3: Inclusion

If students don't respond to the second level of interventions, then it may be necessary to test them to see whether they qualify for special services. Once a student qualifies for special education, all interventions must coincide with the student's Individual Education Plan (IEP). Full inclusion with assistance from members of the special education team is a top priority. The goal of Level 3 is to teach the same knowledge and skills other students are learning, but to allow struggling students to practice these skills at their instructional level (Vygotsky, 1978). As a result, the rigor of assignments and assessments may be modified, or alternate programs may be used to assist students. Under these circumstances, resource teachers are held accountable for setting student goals, administering periodic assessments, monitoring student progress, individualizing instruction, and collecting a body of evidence as described in Chapter 5.

Level 4: Pullout

If students consistently fail to respond to interventions made at the first three levels, they may ultimately be placed in a pullout program with the goal of being mainstreamed as soon as possible. This decision must be made by the Building Intervention Team (a team composed of the student's parents, building administrator, classroom teacher, and other specialists) and must coincide with the laws and regulations of special education.

Each level of intervention contains a diagram of the instructional process described in Step 3 of this chapter. Classroom and resource teachers use best practices to present information, assess student understanding, diagnose learning difficulties, and then intervene. Although the interventions may look different at each level, the instructional process remains the same.

The arrows in the diagram (Figure 6.1) show the best option for interventions, depending on student needs. One problem with public education is that once students are labeled with a learning disability, it can be difficult to remove this label. As a result, students tend to get stuck at a certain level of the intervention process, which fosters dependency. For this reason, it is important to offer the assistance students need and then promote the highest degree of independence possible.

Collegiality holds the intervention process together. As teachers increase their awareness of student needs and as they exhaust their repertoire of strategies, educators rely on one another to provide assistance to students.

Step 6: Hold all educators accountable for student progress.

Administrators must hold teachers accountable for identifying students with learning difficulties and for making timely interventions. Accountability can be accomplished through documentation and personal interviews.

Documentation is an important part of accountability. Whenever student performance on a periodic assessment triggers the intervention process, as described in Steps 1 and 2 of this chapter, teachers should begin a running record that documents concepts students struggle with, when the difficulties occurred, specific strategies used to intervene, and new practices teachers are learning in an attempt to improve their ability to assist students. Teachers should not be allowed to refer students to the next level of the intervention process without showing documentation that proves they have used a variety of best practices to encourage student success. Also, when students do not meet grade-level expectations on state tests, teachers should be required to provide documentation that proves they were aware of learning difficulties prior to end-of-year testing and provided timely assistance to these students.

Individual teacher interviews with the building principal are another important part of accountability. Ideally, principals should meet with teachers at least once a trimester. The first two interviews of the school year allow administrators to determine whether teachers are aware of their students' needs and are making timely interventions. At this time, teachers share documentation that supports their claims to promote student success. The third interview gives teachers an opportunity to explain their students' performance on state tests and to set achievement goals for the next group of students. This interview also gives supervisors an opportunity to provide teachers with recognition privately. When principals use sincere praise to acknowledge characteristics that distinguish teachers, they demonstrate an awareness of and appreciation for the work teachers do. When teachers are not performing as they should, principals can use interviews to develop plans to provide additional assistance.

Step 7: Focus attention on advanced students.

Winebrenner (2001) describes advanced students as "those who have ability in one or more learning areas that exceeds grade/age level expectations by two years or more" (p. 9). These students learn new materials faster than their peers, remember what they have learned, are able to deal with abstract problems that are too complex for peers of the same age, have a passionate interest in one or more topics, or can process more than one task at a time (Winebrenner, 2001). Because effective teachers make special accommodations for struggling students, it stands to reason that teachers should make adjustments for advanced students as well.

Teachers can use a variety of strategies in the regular classroom to meet the needs of advanced students—strategies that require minimal resources and can be implemented with little or no planning on the teachers' part. For example, Winebrenner (2001) suggests ways to compact the curriculum; use learning contracts; develop study guides; create learning centers; capitalize on cooperative learning; provide time to study topics of personal interest; differentiate reading, writing, and math instruction; manage differentiated instruction; encourage students to set personal goals; and track progress.

Fusion is another strategy that can help meet advanced learners' needs. Educators begin the process by identifying the core curriculum students are expected to learn. Next, they decide which curricula have instructional materials available that students could use for independent study. To explain, many textbooks provide instruction, illustrate how to apply new concepts, and offer practice problems that enable students to refine their skills. Curriculum that teachers feel comfortable allowing advanced students to study on their own or in small groups is placed on a Menu of Alternatives similar to Figure 6.3. Students choose a topic, complete the course work, and then take the periodic assessment. These tests are placed into student binders, providing teachers with documentation that advanced students have mastered grade-level standards.

Figure 6.3 Student Menu of Alternatives

Personal Interest	Science	History	Language Arts	Math
People • Abraham Lincoln *Places* • Great Wall of China *Animals* • Dinosaurs *Careers* • Engineering *Transportation* • F-16 jets *Technology* • Podcasts	*Rocks and Minerals* • Identifying minerals • Types of rocks • How rocks are formed • Useful rocks and minerals *Solar System* • The sun • Solar eclipse • Planets and orbits	*Geography* • Mountains • Rivers • Grassland *Mountain Men* • John Colter • Jim Bridger • Jed Smith • Jim Beckwourth *Famous Forts* • Fort Laramie • Fort Bridger	*Reading* • Prefixes/suffixes • Story elements *Mechanics* • Capitalization • Punctuation • Commas • Quotation marks *Usage* • Verbs • Adjectives, adverbs, homophones	*Graphs* • Pictographs • Bar graphs • Line graphs • Circle graphs *Geometry* • Polygons • Symmetry • Flips, slides, turns • Solids • Points, lines, segments, rays, angles

Another alternative is to allow high-ability students to take periodic assessments before completing the course work. If test scores indicate that students have a clear understanding of the content, teachers may decide to allow them to skip the assignments. If periodic assessments are not available, students are allowed more freedom to demonstrate what they have learned. For example, if a student has been learning about John Colter, she could demonstrate her understanding by writing a report, making a poster, creating a display, or using a variety of other techniques that involve higher-order thinking skills.

Once high-ability students have demonstrated mastery of an item on the Student Menu of Alternatives, they are allowed to study topics of personal interest while their peers receive instruction from the teacher. Let's say Becky is a student with advanced math skills but is average in reading and writing. As a result, she is able to learn geometry concepts in two days while the rest of the class requires two weeks. During the geometry unit, Becky works on a personal project in which she uses historical facts to create a model of a Nez Percé village. However, she joins the rest of the class for reading and writing instruction.

Some educators may feel it is unfair to provide advanced students with learning opportunities their peers do not have. One way to involve all students with self-directed learning is through the use of sustained silent reading (Marzano, 2004, pp. 42–61). Students begin by brainstorming topics of personal interest. With their teacher's help, they locate reading material to learn more about their topic of interest. Students are provided with 20- to 30-minute sessions of uninterrupted time to read. Next, students write about or represent the information they learn in academic notebooks using linguistic and nonlinguistic representations. Then they interact with the information by sharing what they have learned with others. Thus, sustained silent reading allows all students, regardless of their ability, to engage in self-directed learning activities.

Classroom management is likely another concern educators may have about differentiating instruction. For the most part, advanced students are quite easy to manage when they are engaged in topics of personal interest or activities that require higher levels of thinking. Teachers can avoid behavioral problems by establishing rules and procedures, clearly stating their expectations, modeling the expected behaviors, and then following through when students misbehave. Students who demonstrate the capacity to use their time productively are allowed more freedom to study independently; whereas students who waste time, distract others, cheat, or make derogatory statements to nonparticipants simply lose this privilege until they prove they can behave responsibly.

Teachers may also be concerned about how to structure students' time for independent study. One teacher-directed option is for the classroom teacher to provide extension activities for students. This option has its benefits, but it requires more planning on the teacher's part, which may discourage her from differentiating instruction. An alternative is student directed: students are encouraged to develop their own projects by brainstorming topics of personal interest, identifying resources that will help them with their studies, using linguistic and nonlinguistic representations to help them process information, and sharing what they have learned with others. As students identify topics of personal interest and resources that facilitate learning, this information is added to the "personal interest" column of the Student Menu of Alternatives. Over time, students have the potential to generate a wealth of resources that add enrichment to the classroom without detracting from the core curriculum or requiring extensive planning by the teacher.

Connecting Fusion with Best Practices

Fusion offers schools a consistent, systematic approach to student interventions. Common formative assessments, indicators that trigger the intervention process, flowcharts, documentation, and personal interviews with administrators increase consistency.

Fusion makes every effort to provide classroom teachers with the skills and assistance they need to include students with special needs in a regular classroom environment.

Fusion helps meet the needs of advanced students by offering them a menu of alternatives and then allowing them to engage in small-group or independent study. This adjusts the pace of instruction, capitalizes on learning style strengths, and uses peer interactions to maximize learning (Winebrenner, 2001).

From Our School to Yours

The Power of Inclusion

We have experimented with inclusion and pullout models. For the most part, students with special needs seem to experience more growth by remaining in the regular classroom and receiving additional assistance from support staff than they do in a pull-out model. This success may be attributed to several factors (Idol, 2006). Classroom teachers maintain high expectations for students with special needs. Classroom teachers and paraprofessionals have also mastered the same strategies, allowing them to work together to differentiate instruction. Paraprofessionals have been trained to look for indicators of off-task behavior and then engage distracted students without interrupting the flow of instruction. Also, we have made an extended effort to use different paraprofessionals with special education students so that they do not become overly dependent on one individual. Equally important, inclusion seems to help students with disabilities develop the social skills needed to interact with peers. It also helps students without disabilities better understand and appreciate individuals who are different from themselves. As a result, we have found inclusion to benefit all students, not just those with special needs.

Occasionally, there are situations when inclusion does not fully meet the needs of some students. Under these circumstances, we use a combined model where students receive instruction in a classroom setting and then are pulled out for 15 or 20 minutes each day for remediation. For example, students that struggle with reading fluency or comprehension are pulled out of the classroom for several minutes each day where they receive additional instruction and practice. As students improve, they graduate from this pullout program.

How Enrichment Can Benefit All Students

Educators at Osmond Elementary worked together with a group of parents to extend learning for students. Funding through the 21st Century Community Learning Centers grants were used to organize after-school activities that provided enrichment and remediation. At the conclusion of the school day, students went to a different teacher's classroom where they received assistance on homework and academic concepts they found difficult. After 45 minutes, students attended enrichment activities of personal choice. These activities included knitting, wood shop, scrapbooking, leatherwork, iPhoto, iMovies, archery, tying fishing flies, Spanish, Native American history, Readers' Theatre, snowshoeing, cross-country skiing, biking, and first aid training. We have found that regardless of their academic ability, students enjoy these enrichment opportunities.

Using Percentages from Formative Assessments to Trigger the Intervention Process

I recommend using formative assessment results rather than grades to trigger the intervention process. Sometimes grades are a reflection of student behavior instead of an indicator of student mastery of state standards. Students may understand the content but, due to excessive absences or negligence in completing classroom assignments, still receive failing grades. Also, variations among teachers' perceptions of high-quality student work make grades inconsistent. One teacher might deem student work to be exceptional, whereas another teacher would consider the same work as mediocre. Finally, it is fairly simple for teachers to pad or adjust grades by assigning extra credit or changing the value of assignments. Common formative assessment, if developed as outlined in Chapter 5, avoids these inconsistencies.

Teaching Students to Use Time Allocated for Independent Study

The old adage "Give a man a fish and you feed him for a day; teach a man to fish and you feed him for a lifetime" is applicable to education. For years, the purpose of education has been to "feed" students information. Student success is often based on the ability to regurgitate information educators deem important. However, society needs creative thinkers, not passive listeners. Rather than fostering student dependency on teachers, educators need to "teach students how to fish" by focusing more attention on metacognitive skills that encourage them to become independent thinkers. Schools must also allow students to take more control of their learning. For this reason, I suggest making metacognitive strategies an integral part of the curriculum and then encouraging students to use these skills when they engage in independent study.

Scenario

Mrs. Kasahara felt pleased with the results of the reading periodic assessment her students completed yesterday. For the most part, her class demonstrated a clear understanding of how to use prefixes, suffixes, and root words to decode difficult vocabulary and to improve reading comprehension. However, Mrs. Kasahara is concerned about Jon and Rachel.

Jon scored 60 percent on the reading test. Based on his pre-test performance, he should have scored at least 75 percent. Knowing this performance triggers the intervention process, Mrs. Kasahara referred to the flowchart her grade-level team had recently created to get ideas for what she could do to help Jon. To begin, she evaluated her approach to instruction. Mrs. Kasahara had used linguistic and nonlinguistic representations, kinesthetic activity, peer discussion, and games to reinforce the concept of affixes and root words. Honestly, she doesn't know what more she can do to teach these concepts. Next, Mrs. Kasahara attempted to diagnose the problem by determining whether attention was an issue. As far as she could tell, Jon was attentive to instruction. However, just to make sure, she invited Ms. Hancock to come to her classroom and conduct an on-task and off-task behavior analysis. The results of the analysis showed that Jon demonstrated passive off-task behaviors during much of instruction. He also relied heavily on the peer sitting next to him to help him complete his work. This information caused Mrs. Kasahara to reconsider the seating arrangement. She had purposely grouped students heterogeneously in an attempt to encourage peer tutoring. Perhaps this peer was providing too much of a crutch for Jon. Mrs. Kasahara decided to make a simple intervention by seating Jon next to a student with a similar reading ability in an attempt to encourage him to pay more attention to instruction. She also decided to contact Jon's parents to see if they would allow him to join an after-school study group for a couple of days so he could receive remedial instruction regarding affixes and root words.

Mrs. Kasahara is also concerned about Rachel. She is an advanced reader who has scored 100 percent on every reading test so far this year. Out of curiosity, Mrs. Kasahara allowed Rachel to take the next periodic assessment as a pre-test. Sure enough, she scored 100 percent. At first, this performance alarmed Mrs. Kasahara. Obviously, Rachel was not benefiting from classroom instruction. Rather than ignoring her needs as a learner, Mrs. Kasahara gave Rachel an interest survey and discovered that she wanted to study ancient civilizations—specifically, Egypt. Next, Rachel signed a student contract specifying behavioral and performance expectations for independent study. She wants to demonstrate her learning by creating a display that provides a brief history of ancient pyramids. Mrs. Kasahara also made arrangements with the media specialist to assist Rachel in finding resources that could help her learn more about Egypt. For the next two weeks, Rachel will learn about Egypt while the rest of the class studies story elements. Her peers do not feel resentment toward Rachel because Mrs. Kasahara has taken the time to create a classroom culture that celebrates diversity. Besides, students interested in Egypt can study this topic during sustained silent reading.

Differentiated Instruction

*How do you encourage teachers to incorporate higher-order
thinking activities into differentiated units of instruction
without fragmenting the curriculum?*

One neat thing about kindergarten students is that they usually
come to school with a sparkle in their eyes, eager to learn. Wouldn't
it be nice if high school seniors shared the same enthusiasm?
Somewhere between kindergarten and graduation, many students
seem to lose their love for learning. The same can be said about
new teachers and those preparing for retirement. Most teachers enter the profession with a strong passion for the content
area they teach and a determination to make a difference in the
lives of students. It doesn't take long, however, for teachers to
discover that compliance is often valued more than creativity.
This is unfortunate because "most teachers—when trusted, when
given time and money, and when given the assistance, choice,
and responsibility to develop curricula—will make extraordinarily
sound decisions about what students should be taught" (Glickman
et al., 2004, p. 405). How can schools encourage teachers to put
enjoyment back into learning without jeopardizing the curriculum?

Scenario

Trent is a typical freshman. His interests include sports, music,
computer games, food, and, of course, girls. Even though Trent
maintains a GPA of 3.7, school isn't necessarily his favorite thing
to do. Take science, for instance. Trent would love to dissect

animals, mix chemicals, and conduct experiments. Instead, he listens to lectures, reads textbooks, and answers questions. To illustrate a typical science class, Trent finds himself at his desk by 8:30 a.m. when the bell rings. The next five minutes are spent doodling while the teacher, Mr. Levin, takes roll. Then the teacher stands before the class and states the objective, "Students, today we will learn about mitosis." Meanwhile, Trent continues to doodle in his notebook. Mr. Levin begins his lecture and writes the same notes he has used for the past 25 years on the whiteboard as he speaks. Several groans are heard as students take out their notebooks and begin copying the information.

For 30 long minutes Mr. Levin drones on and on about mitosis, as if he were carrying on a conversation with himself, while Trent anxiously glances at the clock. Occasionally, the teacher asks a question to ensure that students haven't fallen asleep. The know-it-alls respond to his inquiries, allowing Trent to daydream about the upcoming football game instead of focusing on the discussion. When asked why they were learning about mitosis, Mr. Levin responded that students need to know this information for the test on Friday and that some day this knowledge will be useful. Unfortunately, Trent, who is interested in becoming an attorney, doesn't care about Friday's test and doubts that mitosis will make him a better lawyer.

At the end of the lesson, Mr. Levin instructs his students to turn to page 58 in outdated textbooks, read the chapter, and answer the questions in preparation for tomorrow's lecture on meiosis.

Within 10 minutes the bell rings, and Trent gathers his things and plods to his next class, where he listens to Ms. Jasperson lecture about circumference.

Implementing Fusion

Step 1: Adopt a tiered curriculum.

Most schools consist of educators ranging from novice to veteran teachers. As a result, tasks that are rudimentary to one teacher require great effort from another. For example, learning how to manage a classroom and trying to grasp a district's curriculum are perhaps the greatest challenges for new teachers, but they may not be a big deal for veteran teachers. For this reason, schools should adopt a curriculum that matches teachers' developmental needs. The first tier could emphasize the use of textbooks, the second tier could stress the application of best practices, and the third tier could encourage expert teachers to develop engaging curriculum. The use of formative assessment (see Chapter 5) allows districts to be flexible with curricular issues while maintaining a guaranteed and viable curriculum.

The first tier of the curriculum provides textbooks that could form the basis of instruction, if needed. New teachers naturally rely on textbooks for curricula because they assume adopted textbooks cover state and district standards and teachers' manuals simplify teaching. For this reason, districts must carefully select quality textbooks that provide a solid core curriculum. Also, because textbooks usually cover more content than instructional time allows, educators should provide guidelines that inform new teachers about which information should be emphasized and which information is not considered important or will be taught at a different grade level. Teachers new to the school or district then avoid spending valuable time teaching content that is not essential.

To illustrate, Mr. Sarkowsky is a novice history teacher who has been recently hired. Knowing how demanding the first year of teaching can be, Mrs. Hatch, the principal, assigns a mentor teacher to help him get off to a good start. Before the school year begins, the mentor hands Mr. Sarkowsky two books: *How to Be an Effective Teacher the First Days of School* (Wong & Wong, 2005) to help him with classroom management, and a teacher's manual that accompanies a classroom set of history books to help him with instruction. Mrs. Hatch also provides him with a curriculum map that tells him which chapters to teach along with a time line designed to help teachers pace instruction. Together, Mr. Sarkowsky and his mentor work to identify classroom rules and procedures, and develop lesson plans for the first few days of school.

The second tier of the curriculum encourages teachers to elaborate on textbook instruction by incorporating best practices they learn through Fusion. Back to our example, about midway through his second year of teaching, Mr. Sarkowsky feels more comfortable with classroom management and the content he is expected to teach. As a result, he spends more time studying best practices. As he learns new strategies, he improves his ability to identify situations where they may be applied. For example, last week he taught students about the three branches of government. Recognizing this as an opportunity to identify similarities and differences, Mr. Sarkowsky taught students how to use a comparison matrix to compare the executive, judicial, and the legislative branches of government. This learning activity replaced the assignment given last year where students simply answered the questions at the end of the chapter.

The third tier of the curriculum encourages experienced teachers to develop curricula. Master teachers work together to integrate the strategies they have learned through Fusion into organized units of instruction. For instance, now after six years of teaching, Mr. Sarkowsky has mastered 25 instructional strategies. Although he doesn't consider himself to be an expert, he feels ready to work with master teachers in his department to design classroom curriculum. Using state and district standards to guide this process, he and his colleagues integrate multiple resources into thematic units of instruction. Textbooks are considered to be a valuable resource, but they are no longer the sole curriculum they once were during Mr. Sarkowsky's first year of teaching.

Step 2: Provide guidelines that encourage teachers to develop quality units of instruction.

Chapter 1 describes a Menu of Alternatives designed to encourage teachers to master research-based instructional strategies, proven classroom management techniques, and ways to increase the effectiveness of assessment. The development of curriculum is another important category on this menu. Teachers complete Level 1 and earn a stipend of $250 for developing a unit that has been preapproved by administrators and meets the criteria out-lined in the remainder of this chapter. An additional $250 may be earned for providing evidence that they have actually taught this information to students. Teachers who use instructional units developed through Fusion for two consecutive years meet the requirements for Level 2 and earn 20 points toward a permanent salary increase.

Another alternative is for teachers to incorporate existing units of instruction that meet this criterion and have been approved by administrators. For example, Roger Taylor is well known by educators throughout the United States and Canada for his inte-grated, interdisciplinary model for developing curriculum (Taylor, 2009). Educators from these countries have posted thousands of thematic units on Taylor's Web site that can be downloaded by other teachers. Educators could earn a $250 stipend for teach-ing a thematic unit found on this site. If they use the unit for two consecutive years, they could earn 10 points toward a permanent increase in pay.

The remainder of this section presents the criteria for devel-oping curriculum and a brief description of what is expected of teachers.

Requirements for a Fusion-Friendly Curriculum

1. Enhance personal knowledge.

• The teacher has recently (within the past three years) gained a more in-depth understanding of the content area using resources that have been approved by the teacher facilitator, building administrator, or district personnel. Perhaps the best way to encourage students to become independent, lifelong learners is for adults to model these behaviors themselves. For this reason, the first requirement is for teachers to prove they have recently gained a more in-depth understanding of the content they are teaching. For instance, books, professional journals, videos, work-shops, university courses, and experiences that enhance back-ground knowledge such as visiting historical sites or museums are examples of ways teachers could meet this requirement.

• The teacher represents information using linguistic and nonlinguistic representations. Requiring teachers to use linguistic and nonlinguistic representations (Marzano et al., 2001b) to document what they learn not only enhances long-term memory but also encourages them to incorporate what they have learned into classroom instruction. For example, a science teacher developing a unit on cells could use the combination note-taking approach (Marzano et al., 2001b), which uses written words and visual representations, to record information he or she learns about the latest research on cloning.

2. Deliver quality instruction.

• The teacher uses state and district standards to assist with writing learning goals for the unit. Standards and benchmarks provide a framework for the development of learning goals and activities. Because teachers will be earning financial incentives, it stands to reason that they should be able to easily identify how the units of instruction developed through Fusion correlate with state and district standards.

• The teacher designs instruction in a manner that provides students with multiple, varied exposures to each learning goal and incorporates higher-order thinking skills through the use of questioning techniques and problem-solving activities. An important goal of Fusion is to motivate teachers to focus on an in-depth study of fewer topics rather than a superficial coverage of many topics. Incorporating questioning techniques and problem-solving activities that require higher-order thinking skills into their lessons helps accomplish this goal. For example, rather than having students memorize the definition of inertia and then moving on to a new concept, a science teacher could use a simple experiment where students place an egg on a model car and observe what happens when the car hits an obstacle at the bottom of a ramp. After explaining this example of inertia, students could engage in analysis by completing a Venn diagram that compares and contrasts the egg experiment with automobile collisions. Requiring students to use original thinking to design multiple ways to prevent the egg from rolling off the model car would help them synthesize what they have learned about Newton's First Law. Finally, students could engage in the highest level of Bloom's taxonomy (Bloom, 1956) by using criteria and data to support an argument regarding whether individuals should be required to wear seat belts. Throughout this learning process, the teacher could ask inferential questions (Marzano, Norford, Paynter, Pickering, & Gaddy, 2001a) such as "At what point in history did Newton discover the First Law of Motion," "What danger might inertia present to things or people?" or "What is the value of this experiment?" Of course, activities such as these require time and planning. However, if something is worth teaching, it should be worth teaching well.

• The teacher provides direct vocabulary instruction for key terms. The purpose of this requirement is to encourage teachers to extend vocabulary instruction beyond simply having students copy definitions from a dictionary or a glossary. Marzano (2004) suggests a six-step process that provides students with multiple and varied exposures to important academic terms. Active Process Vocabulary Instruction (Rupley et al., 1998) is another method teachers may use to improve the quality of vocabulary instruction.

• The teacher provides enrichment and remediation. Most classes have students with mixed abilities and interests who require enrichment or remediation. The goal of this requirement is to encourage teachers to consider the needs of their high-performing and low-performing students. Thinking about ways to provide enrichment and remediation as well as gathering the necessary resources prior to presenting new concepts to students increases the likelihood teachers will differentiate instruction.

• The teacher provides opportunities for students to connect new knowledge with real-life application. Educators often neglect to associate the information taught in school with life outside the classroom. How can we expect students to get motivated about learning when the information they study has no real meaning to them? Field trips, simulations, guest speakers, and virtual experiences using the Internet are some ways teachers can make learning more meaningful.

• The teacher models a minimum of three learning activities for other teachers. A recurring theme throughout this book has been the need for teachers to learn from their peers. A transition from learning to use instructional techniques to improving curriculum is the epitome of peer observation.

3. Measure student progress.

• The teacher sets learning goals with individual students and helps them measure progress toward accomplishing these goals. Teachers must encourage students to set personal goals that correspond with the unit and then provide ways for students to track progress as they master these goals. Teachers could use an approach similar to that explained in Chapter 5 by administering a pre-test, using the results of this test to establish a predetermined standard, and then recognizing students for meeting this standard. Another alternative is for students to set personal learning goals and then graph their progress toward meeting these goals, based on rubrics or scales created by the teacher or student (Marzano, 2007).

• The teacher develops or revises a summative assessment that is aligned with state and district standards, measures student mastery of the key concepts of the unit, matches the level of learning required of students, and has a reasonable balance between low-level and high-level questions. Developing content through Fusion requires teachers to move beyond textbook teaching. As a result, teachers will likely need to modify existing assessments or create new tests to ensure that they correlate with the curriculum. They must establish a reasonable balance between low-level and high-level questions (i.e., those with one right answer vs. those with open-ended responses). For example, if the focus of a unit is on rocks and minerals, a low-level question might be "Name the three types of rocks." Simple recall is the cognitive process required to answer this question. A high-level question might be "Explain how a sudden shortage in copper might influence the economy." To answer this question, students would need to understand what copper is and how it is used, and they would need to analyze how its absence would influence the economy—tasks requiring cognitive processes that go beyond simple recall. Obviously, if students haven't participated in higher-order learning activities that required them to analyze the relationship between copper and the economy, the second question would be unfair. For this reason, teachers need to make sure test items match the level of learning required of students.

Another alternative is to ask students to create projects that illustrate their understanding of key concepts. For example, students could create a display showing the different types of rocks and minerals, how they are formed, what they are used for, and so on. After presenting this information to the class, students could answer questions asked by their peers. This cumulative project could take the place of a traditional paper-and-pencil test.

• The teacher develops or revises a minimum of five formative assessments that measure student progress toward mastery of learning goals. Formative assessment can be as simple as documenting students' level of understanding while playing an academic game, checking students' academic notebooks (Marzano, 2004) to assess their knowledge of important concepts, having students complete a performance task, or asking students to articulate their understanding of a concept while the teacher uses a rubric to assess the responses. Formative assessment can also be used in the form of traditional paper-and-pencil quizzes. As long as teachers document the use of at least five formative assessments that enable students to track progress toward meeting learning goals, they have met this requirement.

• The teacher develops or revises scoring rubrics or scales that determine how assessments and other assignments will be scored. Scoring rubrics inform students of teacher expectations and help teachers provide students with objective feedback. Rubrics can be a simple scale with general descriptors of student performance, or they can be more detailed, providing sample responses to test items or student assignments. The teacher decides which type of rubric to use.

4. Organize resources into a unit binder.

- The teacher presents a unit binder to the teacher facilitator and building administrator that contains
  - a label indicating the name of the unit;
  - a table of contents;
  - an outline that includes the purpose of the unit, state and district standards that are addressed, and learning goals and objectives taught in the unit;
  - a student syllabus with information regarding assignments and assessments students are expected to complete, when they are due, and how they will be graded;
  - a hard copy of all teacher and student resources and materials needed for the entire unit, including lesson plans, assessments, assignments, scoring rubrics, and materials for enrichment and remediation (when this is not feasible, such as in situations where the teacher needs to check materials out from the library or when learning activities are Internet based, a reference to where the resources and materials can be located is required);
  - teacher reflections for the unit as a whole (i.e., simple notes describing which lessons worked well and which need to be modified).

The last requirement is fairly self-explanatory. Once teachers have organized and compiled the resources, they present the unit of instruction to the teacher facilitator and building administrator along with student work samples proving they have used these resources to teach students. If the unit meets the Fusion criteria, the teacher is rewarded with a stipend as explained at the beginning of this section. Although the amount of the stipend does not fully compensate teachers for the amount of time required to develop units of instruction, at least it acts as a small token of appreciation for teachers' willingness to improve their students' educational experience.

Step 3: Provide a structure that facilitates the development of curriculum.

Creating high-quality units of instruction is more feasible when teachers have a structure or framework that guides this process. Since there are various frameworks available, teachers should be allowed to choose which structure works best for them. For example, Madeline Hunter (1989) is renowned for her guide to developing lesson plans. As mentioned previously, Roger Taylor (2009) offers a framework on his Web site that assists teachers with organizing thematic units. Teachers could also use Bloom's taxonomy (Bloom, 1956) as a guide to help them develop curriculum.

Another alternative is to provide teachers with a framework that allows them to synthesize best practices. Appendix B provides examples of lesson plan organizers developed at our school for the purpose of helping teachers incorporate strategies discussed in *Classroom Instruction That Works: Research-Based Strategies for Increasing Student Achievement* (Marzano et al., 2001b), *Building Background Knowledge for Academic Achievement* (Marzano, 2004), *Building Academic Vocabulary: Teacher's Manual* (Marzano & Pickering, 2005), and *The Art and Science of Teaching* (Marzano, 2007). Obviously, teachers will not use every strategy listed in this organizer but rather choose strategies that are most suitable to the learning situation. Also, lessons may take more than one class period to complete. The helpfulness of this organizer depends on teachers' ability to employ the strategies listed. For this reason, schools are encouraged to emphasize the mastery of best practices the first two or three years they implement Fusion and then concentrate on the improvement of classroom curriculum.

Step 4: Provide time for teachers to develop units of instruction.

It is important for schools to provide time during contract hours for teachers to develop curriculum. I suggested in Chapter 4 that teachers need at least 15 minutes each day to read and respond to professional literature, two hours every three weeks to collaborate with colleagues in study groups, two days each week to participate in peer observation, and traditional planning time to prepare lesson plans and evaluate student work.

Time allocated for Fusion can be used to create units of instruction. For example, some teachers may choose to use the two hours set aside for study groups to develop curriculum rather than to study best practices. Another option is to make entire workdays available for teachers to develop curriculum. This alternative provides teachers with more time to prepare materials while the ideas are fresh on their minds. A third alternative is for districts to offer workshops that facilitate the development of curriculum. For example, teachers could sign up to participate in a weeklong workshop at the beginning or near the end of the summer. Districts could have personnel readily available who specialize in technology or the use of best practices, or who understand how to develop thematic units of instruction. These individuals could offer suggestions to teachers and help them locate resources. At the end of the workshop, teachers who had developed units that met Fusion's criteria would receive a stipend.

Step 5: Encourage teachers to work collaboratively.

Fusion encourages grade-level or content area teachers to work collaboratively to create units of instruction. Working together reduces the amount of time it takes to develop curricula, capitalizes on teachers' strengths, increases instructional consistency, and improves the quality of the finished product.

From Our School to Yours

Lasting School Improvement

It has taken longer than we anticipated for our school to progress to this phase of the improvement process. We are now in the initial stages of developing curriculum as outlined in this chapter.

How Enriched Background Knowledge Enhances Learning

One requirement of Fusion is for teachers to prove they have recently gained a more in-depth understanding of their content area. Enhancing background knowledge is a viable way to meet this requirement. For example, a few years ago several colleagues and I had the opportunity to attend a conference in Boston. Although the workshops were fascinating, our visits to historical sites made a lasting impression. I will never forget the cobblestone streets; the sights, sounds, and smells of the marketplace; the Old North Church; Bunker Hill; and Old Iron Sides. One teacher even threw a small pinch of tea leaves into Boston Harbor so that he could tell his students that he had made his contribution to the Boston Tea Party.

Today, when students study the early history of the United States, they enjoy reliving these experiences with their teachers. It would be wonderful if schools had the finances to send all students to places like Boston. Providing teachers with these opportunities is the next best thing but if that also is not possible, even taking virtual tours of museums or other famous sites can be rewarding. Schools should do what they can to give teachers opportunities to enhance their background knowledge.

The Role of Tiered Curriculum in Professional Growth

Osmond Elementary has hired several new teachers over the past few years. The normal reaction is for them to feel inadequate once they see the strategies other educators are using. New teachers typically feel a sense of urgency to try to catch up with their peers, which can be overwhelming. Encouraging novice teachers to focus their attention on classroom management and to rely on textbooks for instruction reduces the anxiety they feel. Then, as teachers feel ready, they learn key strategies and programs that form the basis of our curriculum.

A tiered curriculum has also helped meet the needs of experienced teachers on our staff. Approximately 50 percent of our teachers have taught for more than 20 years. Forcing them to use scripted programs or to base all of their instruction on classroom textbooks would be a great disservice to students. Because every program has its strengths and weaknesses, encouraging experienced teachers to use a combination of programs has improved our curriculum.

Strategy Synthesis with a Lesson Plan Organizer

The organizers represented in Appendix B helped teachers discover inconsistencies in our instruction. As mentioned previously, our school has placed a strong emphasis on mastering the strategies presented in Marzano's work (Marzano, 2004, 2007; Marzano & Pickering, 2005; Marzano et al., 2001b). These strategies improved student learning, but it was difficult for teachers to know at what point in the instructional process to use them. As a result, although we felt fairly confident with our ability to employ these strategies, we did not use them systematically. We also realized that the majority of our teaching was devoted to presenting new information to students instead of allowing them to process what they were learning. We discovered, too, that most teachers were unaware of the differences between declarative and procedural information (Marzano, 2007, pp. 18–19). As a result, learning activities didn't match the type of information students were expected to learn, which explained why students had difficulty remembering what was taught. The lesson plan organizer helped teachers resolve these issues.

Technology as an Effective Mode of Formative Assessment

Activstudio (Pearce, 2009) has a feature that allows information to be projected onto an interactive whiteboard. Students respond using Activotes, or electronic devices that allow the entire class to answer a question simultaneously without saying a word. The computer tallies student responses and displays a bar graph illustrating the percentage of students who selected a particular answer. Student responses are automatically recorded and can be used as a formative assessment, if desired.

Academic Games

Osmond Elementary has recently made an effort to incorporate academic games designed to deepen students' understanding of important vocabulary. To facilitate this process, we held several study group sessions where teachers read and discussed the games described in *Building Academic Vocabulary: Teacher's Manual* (Marzano & Pickering, 2005). Teachers volunteered to experiment with a game and then model it for others. Teachers also shared resources they developed such as PowerPoint presentations and templates that could be used with Activstudio.

Students, regardless of their grade level, seemed to enjoy the variety these games offered to the curriculum. Academic games fostered an environment of cooperation because students had to work together to answer the questions and were motivated to learn the content because they wanted to outperform their peers.

Scenario

Trent wished all of his classes could be like history. For example, two weeks ago, his teacher, Mrs. Rice, set up a simulation that resembled the economy. Students earned fake money by doing their homework, meeting their goals on quizzes and tests, and completing additional assignments that were not required for the course. With this money, students paid taxes, paid rent for their desks, and paid for special privileges such as sharpening a pencil or getting a drink of water. They could use money that was left over as a down payment to purchase their desk or to procure the desks of other students, who then had to pay rent to the landlord. Another option was to invest additional money in the stock market or to place it in the bank. Students earned interest for investments they made and paid interest for taking out loans or purchasing items with credit. Deposits and expenditures were tracked on spreadsheets, and students were fined for calculation errors.

Trent was one of the first in his class to catch on to this simulation. As a result, he made a small fortune buying and selling stock. In fact, Trent soon had enough money to purchase his desk as well as the desks of four of his classmates. Life was great—until last Tuesday, when the stock market crashed and Trent lost everything. With a smile on her face, Mrs. Rice handed out a book called *The Grapes of Wrath* and cheerfully welcomed her students to the Great Depression. Needless to say, Trent is always curious about what he will be learning next in Mrs. Rice's class.

Change Through Fusion

Are you ready to apply the principles of Fusion?

Albert Einstein is reported to have defined insanity as "doing the same thing over and over again and expecting different results." This advice applies to educational reform as well. How can leaders expect to get different results when they approach school improvement efforts as they have in the past? Recognizing the magnitude of change desired and then adapting leadership techniques to match the order of change increases the likelihood new innovations will succeed.

> First-order change is incremental. It can be thought of as the next most obvious step to take in a school or district. Second-order change is anything but incremental. It involves dramatic departures from the expected, both in defining a given problem and in finding a solution. . . . Incremental change fine-tunes the system through a series of small steps that do not depart radically from the past. Deep change alters the system in fundamental ways, offering a dramatic shift in direction and requiring new ways of thinking and acting. (Marzano, Waters, & McNulty, 2005, p. 66)

Fusion is second-order change. Although the principles of Fusion are simple and straightforward, "it alters the system in fundamental ways, offering a dramatic shift in direction that require new ways of thinking and acting" (Marzano et al., 2005, p. 66). Because the nature of Fusion is so comprehensive, teachers feel overwhelmed if they are exposed to this innovation all at once. For this reason, I suggest implementing Fusion in three separate phases. Phase 1 focuses on building positive relationships within a school while improving instruction. Phase 2 uses formative assessment to increase academic rigor. Phase 3 is designed to make learning relevant by enhancing classroom curriculum.

Phase 1: Building Positive Relationships

Chapters 1 through 4 describe a motivational system designed to enhance professional development. The goal of this phase is to improve relationships, or school culture, by developing professional learning communities where teachers feel comfortable studying best practices together, experimenting with new techniques, engaging in peer observation, and sharing ideas.

Fusion incorporates several strategies to accomplish this goal. Initially, regular time is set aside for teachers to participate in professional development activities. Then, teachers choose instructional practices of personal interest from a Menu of Alternatives. Teachers complete the mastery process in which they study research pertaining to the practice, discuss it in study groups, observe its proficient use based on predetermined criteria, and then demonstrate mastery of the strategy while being observed by a mentor. After completing the mastery process, they receive a small stipend. Teachers who document proficient use of a strategy multiple times across the curriculum earn points toward a permanent increase in pay. Making a clear distinction between formative and summative roles—by allowing teacher leaders to take responsibility for Fusion while administrators complete summative responsibilities—creates a risk-taking atmosphere that promotes professional growth.

The most obvious indicator that Phase 1 is accomplishing its goal is a renewed enthusiasm for teaching. Teachers who get involved with Fusion become excited about professional development and the opportunity to study best practices with their colleagues. Another indicator of success is an increase in peer observation. It is not uncommon for teachers to collectively participate in hundreds of observations. A common professional dialogue becomes more apparent. Leaders will notice spontaneous discussions among teachers regarding best practices, and administrators will see evidence of the use of new instructional strategies when conducting formal and informal evaluations.

Phase 2: Increasing Academic Rigor

Chapters 5 and 6 describe ways educators can use Fusion to increase the productivity of assessment. This phase of the improvement process has several important goals. The first is to increase academic rigor by developing a guaranteed and viable curriculum. Educators work collaboratively to develop common assessments that are formative in nature and match or exceed the rigor of state testing.

Another goal is to motivate teachers and students to take ownership for academic progress through the use of goal setting and timely feedback. Teachers administer a pre-test at the beginning of the year to gather baseline data. According to these data, teachers set achievement goals that not only challenge students to do their best but also reflect their effectiveness as teachers. Throughout the year students take periodic assessments, graph their progress toward reaching their goals, and place this information into student binders. Teachers emphasize the correlation between effort and achievement, and they recognize students who have met their achievement goals.

The final goal of Phase 2 is to create a system of interventions that meets the needs of every student. Flowcharts are used to inform teachers when to instigate the intervention process, reminding them to be considerate of the needs of advanced students and those with special needs. Flowcharts also suggest specific interventions that can be made, making them useful resources for teachers.

Because educators are striving to meet the same rigorous standards, academic consistency indicates that Phase 2 has been successful. Throughout the year, leaders will be able to inquire about the academic performance of any student, and teachers should be able to readily share samples of student work as well as documented attempts to provide timely interventions. Another indicator of success is an increase in student motivation. As teachers differentiate instruction and provide recognition to students for meeting challenging goals, their enthusiasm for school increases. Educators should witness an improvement in standardized test scores near the end of this phase.

Phase 3: Enhancing Academic Relevance

Chapter 7 suggests ways to improve classroom curriculum. In the third and final phase of Fusion, teachers strive to make learning relevant to students by synthesizing the best practices they have learned during the first two phases into organized units of instruction.

The goal of Phase 3 is to motivate teachers and students to become lifelong learners. This is accomplished by adopting a tiered curriculum that meets teachers' developmental needs. Once teachers have learned how to manage a classroom and have become familiar with a district's curriculum, they are encouraged to develop units of instruction that correspond with state and district standards. Teachers are provided with guidelines that encourage them to enhance their personal knowledge, deliver quality instruction, measure student progress, and organize resources into unit binders. Teachers may choose from frameworks that assist them with developing thematic units, organizers that help them synthesize best practices, or other methods educators find useful. Finally, providing teachers with time during contract hours and encouraging them to work collaboratively improve the quality and consistency of classroom curriculum.

The third phase of Fusion will have been successful when leaders observe organized lessons that engage students in higher levels of Bloom's taxonomy. As a result, learning becomes more relevant to students and achievement extends beyond improved test scores to life outside the classroom.

Implementing Fusion

Step 1: Understand your teachers.

Teachers play an important role in second-order change. For this reason, understanding what frustrates teachers, as well as what motivates them, increases a leader's capacity to tap the potential of his or her staff. For example, most teachers feel overwhelmed with the amount of content they are expected to teach and with the increasingly difficult social problems students come to school with. Anything building principals can do to reduce this burden is greatly appreciated by teachers. Teachers feel frustrated when they are expected to jump from one innovation to the next. Carefully researching best practices and then providing teachers with ample time to learn them is helpful. Teachers experience frustration when they go through the motions of shared decision-making, only to find that leaders have previously made the decision. Teachers prefer it when administrators are open and upfront with them. Finally, teachers feel tremendous pressure to prepare students to perform well on state testing. A simple word of encouragement from an administrator can motivate teachers to do better.

Leaders must also understand that teachers on their faculty come with different educational philosophies and beliefs, depending on the university they attended and the trends that were popular at the time (Fullan & Hargreaves, 1996). This helps explain why coming to a consensus can be difficult. For example, there was a time when whole language was considered to be an effective way to teach reading while the use of phonics was discouraged. At other times phonics instruction has been heavily emphasized while the use of whole language was discouraged. Consequently, attempting to unite a faculty in how they approach reading instruction can result in heated debates. Leaders need to understand the different educational philosophies that have been ingrained into teachers and then capitalize on the strengths of these values.

Step 2: Understand your leadership style.

Chapter 3 briefly described how leaders should adjust supervisory behaviors to best meet teachers' developmental needs. There are some situations when leaders should exercise control and other situations when teachers should be allowed to rely on their professional judgment. The ability to apply principles of developmental supervision (Glickman et al., 2004) takes time and practice. Realizing that administrators naturally tend to favor one leadership style more than others can help principals avoid unnecessary personality conflicts with their staff. Glickman & Tamashiro (1980) identified three supervisory beliefs, or styles that correspond with developmental supervision and influence the way leaders interact with teachers.

> Directive Supervision is an approach based on the belief that teaching consists of technical skills with known standards and competencies for all teachers to be effective. The supervisor's role is to inform, direct, model, and assess those competencies.
>
> Collaborative Supervision is based on the belief that teaching is primarily problem solving, whereby two or more persons jointly pose hypotheses to a problem, experiment, and implement those teaching strategies that appear to be the most relevant in their own surroundings. The supervisor's role is to guide the problem-solving process, be an active member of the interaction, and keep the teachers focused on their common problems.
>
> Non-Directive Supervision has as its premise that learning is primarily a private experience in which individuals must come up with their own solutions to improving the classroom experience for students. The supervisor's role is to listen, be nonjudgmental, and provide self-awareness and clarification experiences for teachers. (p. 76)

In essence, leaders who favor directive supervision believe supervisors know what's best and therefore expect teachers to comply. Their motto could very well be "My way or the highway." They place a strong emphasis on schoolwide programs, standardized test scores, evaluation, and accountability. Controlling behaviors contradict the concepts of teacher autonomy and teacher leadership. As a result, Fusion does not thrive in these environments.

Leaders who take a nondirective approach to supervision believe teachers know best how to educate students. As a result, leaders tend to fade into the background, allowing teacher autonomy to govern the school. One could say the philosophy of these leaders reflects the Cheshire cat's advice to Alice in Wonderland: "If you don't know where you are going, any road will take you there." Although leaders who rely on a nondirective style value teacher autonomy, their lack of direction and reluctance to address performance issues can hamper the success of Fusion.

Collaborative supervision values teacher autonomy and accountability. The motto of these leaders could be "How you get there is a choice; getting there is not." Principals who embrace this style of leadership foster a climate that encourages teachers to try new strategies. However, educators also rely on proven methodologies, assessment, and evaluation to ensure that they are meeting students' needs. Leaders encourage independence yet are not afraid to confront teachers who stand in need of correction. Fusion thrives in schools that embrace collaborative supervision.

Step 3: Balance choice with accountability.

This book has placed a strong emphasis on encouraging teacher autonomy, and it has suggested positive ways to hold teachers accountable. The ability to maintain a balance between choice and accountability is a leadership characteristic that is essential to the success of Fusion. Choice is the degree to which individuals are allowed to use their judgment to make important decisions. Accountability is the extent to which individuals are held responsible for the decisions they make. Educators who have been granted a great deal of autonomy should also be held to a higher standard of accountability. Conversely, when freedom to make decisions is taken away, accountability shifts to the individuals who have restricted autonomy. As autonomy increases or decreases, so should accountability. The following scenarios illustrate the value schools can place on choice and accountability.

Schools That Value Choice More Than Accountability

Diversity is a defining characteristic of schools that value teacher autonomy more than accountability. Teachers are allowed freedom to teach what they want and to the extent they want to teach it. As a result, every classroom is unique, which adds variety to students' educational experience. However, the quality of students' education depends largely on the teachers they are assigned. Because pet units usually take precedence, there is no guarantee students will master knowledge and skills deemed essential by the district. Lack of clear standards and expectations make grading inconsistent, and very little correlation exists between grades and student mastery of state standards. Standardized testing is a yearly routine, but little is done with the results. Test scores may be glanced over, but then they are filed away and forgotten. There is no sustained effort to track student progress, question the effectiveness of the school, or set meaningful improvement goals. Although the principal regularly evaluates teachers, these evaluations tend to focus on the positive while ignoring areas that need improvement. As a result, ineffective teachers can coast through an entire career without being held accountable for their actions.

Schools That Value Accountability More Than Choice

Structure is a defining characteristic of schools that value accountability more than choice. In these schools, programs are trusted more than teacher expertise. As a result, teachers are required to teach the same content at the same time and in the same way. Students receive adequate exposure to state standards, but each classroom looks boringly the same. Assessment is strongly emphasized. Teachers feel a constant pressure to improve test scores, so they focus their attention on test-taking skills rather than enrichment. Teachers are afraid to add variety to the curriculum for fear of negative repercussions. Although students will likely master basic skills, the monotony of school destroys creativity and the desire to learn. As a result, students may possess the skills necessary to succeed, but they lack the drive to use them.

Schools That Balance Choice with Accountability

Structured diversity is a characteristic of schools where choice and accountability are balanced. These schools have a strong sense of direction but not a controlled or micromanaged environment. High expectations are a part of daily life, but school is also an enjoyable place to be. Teachers are encouraged to use their professionalism to make learning exciting for students, but not at the expense of knowledge and skills deemed essential. Teachers who demonstrate the ability to help all students progress toward meeting grade-level standards are allowed the freedom to use instructional practices they feel are necessary. Teachers who do not demonstrate this ability are not allowed the same autonomy. Instead, the principal or teacher mentors work closely with these individuals to help them improve. Student progress is based on teachers' judgments as well as common assessments used in each classroom; therefore, grading is consistent across grade levels, and there is a strong correlation between grades and a student's ability to meet state standards. Evaluation is also an important aspect of these schools. Because student learning is the top priority, leaders and teachers are not afraid to address sensitive topics regarding instruction and classroom curriculum. These schools realize that unless you continually challenge the status quo, you will never reach excellence.

In summary, choice and accountability go hand in hand. Schools that allow teachers autonomy and hold them accountable for the choices they make will improve academic achievement. The degree to which teachers choose is the degree to which they should be held accountable. The degree to which administrators and policy makers dictate is the degree to which they should be held accountable. Choice should never outweigh accountability, nor should accountability outweigh choice.

Applying the Principles of Fusion at Your School

The following questions will help you determine whether you are ready to implement Fusion in your school or district.

• **Are you ready to become an expert on Fusion?** Leaders must understand Fusion to the extent that they can clearly articulate it to their colleagues, staff, members of the school board, the public, and state legislators. Administrators must also be able to recognize whether Fusion is being implemented properly, which requires expertise.

• **Are you ready to provide time and resources for Fusion?** One of the greatest challenges leaders face will be finding ways to make time and resources available for Fusion. However, where there is a will, there is a way.

• **Are you ready to provide high-quality training to your faculty?** The success of school reform depends on the momentum new initiatives generate. Proper training provides the spark that ignites the change process. For this reason, high-quality training is vital to the success of Fusion.

• **Are you ready to maintain high expectations for every teacher, regardless of whether they participate in Fusion?** Every teacher should be expected to develop professionally, establish a classroom environment conducive to learning, differentiate instruction, track student progress, make timely interventions, and engage students in higher levels of Bloom's taxonomy regardless of whether they participate in Fusion. Developmental supervision (Glickman et al., 2004) is a tool that can assist leaders with this important responsibility.

• **Are you ready to share instructional leadership responsibilities with teacher leaders?** Allowing teacher facilitators to take responsibility for Fusion gives teachers exposure to instructional leadership roles. However, for this effort to be successful, leaders must maintain open lines of communication, offer moral support, and let facilitators complete their responsibilities without micromanaging them or requiring them to complete administrative duties that extend beyond Fusion.

• **Are you ready to facilitate peer observation?** Some leaders feel uncomfortable with the idea of teachers spending time away from their students to engage in peer observation. Others feel strongly about students being in contact with a certified teacher at all times. This attitude influences the decision schools make when selecting a roaming substitute. Leaders must carefully analyze their feelings regarding peer observation if they want it to thrive at their school.

• **Are you ready to support collaboration?** One way to support collaboration is to maintain a clear distinction between Fusion and traditional faculty meetings. Sometimes leaders take 5 or 10 minutes at the beginning of a Fusion study group session to conduct school business. Usually, 10 minutes turns into half an hour. As a result, teachers normally lose interest in discussing instructional strategies. An important way to support collaboration is to avoid mixing traditional meetings with Fusion.

• **Are you ready to lead through example?** The epilogue provides a brief description of how Fusion can be applied at the administrative level. Are you willing to apply the principles of Fusion to improve your leadership skills?

From Our School to Yours

No Quick-Fix Solutions

Schools that are serious about lasting school improvement have discovered that there are no quick-fix solutions to educational reform. For this reason, schools should plan on at least five years to fully implement Fusion.

The first phase described earlier in this chapter requires approximately two years. The first year teachers work together as a school studying the same strategies, allowing them to become familiar with Fusion. The second year of implementation, teachers branch out into study groups based on personal interest.

The second phase of Fusion may take another two to three years, depending on the number of content areas that schools target. For example, if elementary schools focus on one content area per year, which is recommended, it takes about three years to develop formative assessments for reading, writing, and math. If secondary schools decide to have content area teams work simultaneously, they can reduce the amount of time it takes to complete the second phase of Fusion.

The third phase does not have a time line. Although teachers will engage in all three phases of Fusion throughout their careers, the bulk of their time should be spent incorporating strategies they have learned into units of instruction.

Every Phase of Fusion Is Necessary

Each stage of Fusion adds to educators' capacity to meet students' needs and maximize student achievement. Therefore, it is necessary for schools to advance to the different phases of Fusion; otherwise, they will reach a plateau that limits progression. Because Phase 1 of Fusion focuses on autonomy, it appeals to most teachers, which facilitates the implementation process. Assessment, in Phase 2, is not as appealing, so schools often tend to get stuck at the first phase. Although learning best practices is valuable, developing formative assessments and improving classroom curricula are equally important.

Too Much of a Good Thing?

Fusion is like seasoning: If you don't have enough, food tastes bland. If you have too much, food becomes inedible. However, the right amount of seasoning makes food taste delicious. After implementing Fusion for several years, the frequency of meetings at our school increased. On Wednesdays, the faculty gathered together for lunch. On Thursdays, teachers met for Fusion or for accreditation tasks. On Fridays, grade-level teams met to discuss classroom issues and receive training. Although collaboration can be powerful, meeting together three times a week was too much. As a result, there was a sharp decline in peer observation and the number of strategies teachers mastered through Fusion. Teachers felt overwhelmed with the many tasks required of them, and getting together was no longer special, so they began to lose interest in professional development.

Different Teachers, Different Rates of Progress

It would be convenient if leaders could present Fusion to their faculties and then have their teachers advance concurrently through the three phases of Fusion. One reason second-order change is complicated has to do with it not being a cut-and-dried process. Consequently, schools can expect to have educators at different stages of the change process.

Closing Thoughts

I once heard a story about a memorable meal a family shared together. The main course was soup made from a recipe that had been cherished for generations. As the mother began preparing the meal, each family member privately came to her and requested that one of the ingredients be withheld. The youngest son disliked carrots. A daughter thought onions were repulsive. Another son didn't like potatoes. The husband detested peppers. One by one, ingredients were eliminated from the recipe. At dinnertime, the family assembled around the table, eagerly awaiting their tasty meal. However, this eagerness quickly dissipated as the steamy liquid was served. The attempt to improve the soup by eliminating ingredients resulted in nothing more than a bowl of hot water.

Implementing Fusion is similar to this story. Every change brings a consequence. For example, if the element of choice is eliminated, teachers resist Fusion. If the stipend is removed from the motivational system, teachers tend not to complete the mastery process. If time during the school day is not set aside for Fusion, other priorities prevent participation. If a school has previously adopted approaches to peer mentoring, it may feel inclined to combine these philosophies with Fusion. If teachers are required to provide feedback to their peers, they may resent peer observation. If financial incentives are associated with test results rather than personal improvement, teachers may emphasize test-taking skills rather than best practices. If the teacher facilitator is required to take full responsibility for professional development, study groups may resemble workshops rather than professional learning communities. Every aspect of Fusion has a purpose. Similar to how one tiny electron determines whether sodium and chloride become table salt, small changes determine—that is, change—the dynamics of Fusion.

The preface of this book mentioned that "introducing a seemingly small change can turn out to have wild consequences" (Fullan, 1993, p. viii). Combining time, a motivational system, and teacher leadership has generated a synergy that has improved our school beyond what we imagined possible. Students have ultimately been the greatest beneficiaries of these improvements. Although second-order change has not been easy, it has been worthwhile. Are you willing to become a catalyst of change at your school?

Epilogue
The Versatility of Fusion

•·······································•

The beauty of Fusion is that it's simple and adaptable. The principles of Fusion can be applied in myriad contexts, both in and outside education.

Using Fusion to Determine Teacher Tenure

Fusion can be used as a mentoring program for novice teachers. For example, a district may decide that mastery of fundamental classroom management and instructional skills is necessary for beginning teachers to earn tenure. Novice teachers from various schools within a district meet together with one or two veteran teachers, acting as discussion leaders, to form study groups. New teachers complete the mastery process as outlined in Chapter 2 and receive a stipend once they demonstrate proficiency. Because the purpose of this process is to determine teacher tenure, it is summative in nature. Therefore, the building administrator, rather than the teacher facilitator, determines when new teachers have mastered strategies deemed essential by the district. Once beginning teachers demonstrate the ability to apply these strategies, they earn tenure, regardless of whether this process takes two years or five. After teachers have become tenured, the teacher facilitator, not the building administrator, oversees their participation in Fusion.

Applying Fusion at the Administrative Level

The principles of Fusion can be applied to settings beyond the classroom. At the administrative level, leaders identify strategies that can improve their leadership skills and then add them to a Menu of Alternatives similar to Figure E.1.

Administrators complete a mastery process in which they read professional literature, respond to writing prompts, participate in study groups with other leaders, observe a colleague model a strategy, and then demonstrate the ability to employ what they have studied based on observation/demonstration criteria. After completing Level 1, administrators earn a stipend. Leaders who can prove these strategies have become an integral part of their repertoire of leadership skills earn points that can be used for a permanent increase in pay.

Some leadership skills may be more applicable to the mastery process than others. For example, it would be fairly simple to invite a colleague to attend a faculty meeting to observe a principal incorporate group process skills. However, many leadership skills are applied spontaneously, making it difficult to schedule peer observation. For instance, calming an angry parent or handling an emergency situation requires immediate attention. It would be unreasonable to keep an irate parent waiting while the principal contacts a peer from another building and asks that colleague to come and observe the principal model how to use interpersonal skills to handle the situation. Instead, role playing can be used to complete the mastery process when peer observation is not feasible. One principal could take on the role of an angry parent, while another principal models the ability to address the situation in a competent manner. Even though role playing may feel uncomfortable initially, the practice will benefit both principals the next time they communicate with an upset parent.

Figure E.1 Menu of Alternatives for Administrators

Supervisory Skills	Instructional Leadership Skills	Administrative Skills	Interpersonal Skills	Technological Skills	Leadership Characteristics (Marzano, 2005)
Developmental Supervision	A Guaranteed and Viable Curriculum	Safe and Orderly Environment	Parent and Community Involvement	Designing Web Pages	Optimizer
					Affirmation
Quantitative Observations	Challenging Goals and Effective Feedback	Assessing and Planning Skills	Developing Collaborative Groups	Internet Blogs	Ideals/Beliefs
Qualitative Observations		Designing Time-Efficient and Effective Meetings	Using Conflict as a Resource		Visibility
					Situational Awareness
Tailored Observation Systems			Collegiality and Professionalism		Relationships
					Communication

Using Fusion to Transform Other Professions

Any profession that involves adult learning could apply the principles of Fusion. For example, the medical profession could offer a Menu of Alternatives to nurses and then encourage them to improve their skills through completion of the mastery process. The business community could identify key characteristics that would improve the performance of their business and then use Fusion as a tool to motivate employees to master these skills. Professional trades could also apply the principles of Fusion to improve the training of new apprentices. With a little imagination, the principles of Fusion can be applied to ignite change in a variety of organizations.

Appendix A

· ·

Appendix A   Requirements to Qualify for a Permanent Increase in Pay

Menu of Alternatives	Requirements	Point Value	Example
Strategy	• Complete reading assignment, written responses, observe a mentor, demonstrate proficiency. • Collect nine lesson plans and/or student samples that illustrate proficient use of the strategy across the curriculum.	2	Venn diagram
Classroom Management	• Complete reading assignment, written responses, observe a mentor, demonstrate proficiency. • Provide evidence that the classroom management technique has become embedded in daily proceedings.	3	Rules and Procedures
Technology	• Complete reading assignment, written responses, observe a mentor, demonstrate proficiency. • Collect nine lesson plans and/or student samples that illustrate proficient use across the curriculum.	4	Activstudio

Appendix A *Continued*

Menu of Alternatives	Requirements	Point Value	Example
Assessment	The teacher provides documentation of the use of • a pre- and post-test that is aligned with state standards, comprehensive in nature, and matches or exceeds the rigor of state testing. • a minimum of five periodic assessments that match or exceed the rigor of state testing, measure student progress toward mastery of state and district standards, and prepare students for the post-test. • teacher goals that measure the effectiveness of instruction. These goals are based on students' pre-test performance and must be set for the class as a whole and for student subgroups. The teacher must also use charts or graphs to illustrate student progress toward reaching these goals. • student goals that are individualized, focused on growth, and based on students' pre-test performance. • student binders or portfolios that contain pre- and post-tests, periodic assessments, and charts or graphs that illustrate student goals and progress toward reaching these goals. • strategies that reinforce effort and provide recognition to students when they reach achievement goals. • formative assessment for two consecutive years.	8	Develop formative assessment for the content area of math
Approach	• Complete reading assignments, written responses, observations and demonstrations. • Collect nine lesson plans and/or student samples that illustrate proficient use of the approach across the curriculum.	12	Summarizing and Note Taking
Program (when applicable)	• Complete reading assignments, written responses, observe a mentor, demonstrate proficiency.	16	The 6 + 1 Traits of Writing

Appendix A *Continued*			

Menu of Alternatives	Requirements	Point Value	Example
	• Provide evidence that the teacher has incorporated the program into classroom instruction.		
Content	The teacher • has recently (within the past three years) gained a more in-depth understanding of the content area using resources that have been approved by the teacher facilitator, building administrator, or district personnel. • represents information learned from their studies using linguistic and nonlinguistic representations. • uses state and district standards to assist him or her with writing learning goals for the unit. • designs instruction in a manner that provides students with multiple, varied exposures to each learning goal and incorporates higher-order thinking skills through the use of questioning techniques and problem-solving activities. • provides direct vocabulary instruction for key terms. • provides enrichment and remediation. • provides opportunities for students to connect new knowledge with real-life application. • models a minimum of three learning activities for other teachers. • sets learning goals with individual students and helps them measure progress toward accomplishing these goals. • develops and/or revises a summative assessment that is aligned with state and district standards, measures student mastery of the key concepts of the unit, matches the level of learning required of students, and has a reasonable balance between low-level and high-level questions.	20	A unit on westward expansion

Appendix A *Continued*			

Menu of Alternatives	Requirements	Point Value	Example
	• develops and/or revises a minimum of five formative assessments that measure student progress toward mastery of learning goals. • develops and/or revises scoring rubrics or scales that determine how assessments and other assignments will be scored. • presents a unit binder to the teacher facilitator and building administrator that contains – a label indicating the name of the unit; – a table of contents; – an outline that includes the purpose of the unit, state and district standards that are addressed, and learning goals and objectives taught in the unit; – a student syllabus with information regarding assignments and assessments students are expected to complete, when they are due, and how they will be graded; – a hard copy of all teacher and student resources and materials needed for the entire unit including lesson plans, assessments, assignments, scoring rubrics, and materials for enrichment and remediation (when this is not feasible, a reference to where the resources and materials can be located is required); – teacher reflections for the unit as a whole.		
Miscellaneous	Teachers earn an additional 10 points (for a total of 75 points) by selecting instructional practices of personal interest.	10	Metaphors, Analogies, T-R-I Frame, Mental Images, Carrying Out Discipline Actions

Appendix B

Lesson Plan Organizers

Appendix B.1   Integrating Standards and Benchmarks with Learning Goals

Name of Unit:

State Standard(s):

Benchmark(s):

Learning Goal 1:

(Students will understand___. Students will be able to___. Students will understand___ and be able to___.)

Learning Goal 2:

(Students will understand___. Students will be able to___. Students will understand___ and be able to___.)

Learning Goal 3:

(Students will understand___. Students will be able to___. Students will understand___ and be able to___.)

Learning Goal 4:

(Students will understand___. Students will be able to___. Students will understand___ and be able to___.)

Learning Goal 5:

(Students will understand___. Students will be able to___. Students will understand___ and be able to___.)

How will I reinforce effort?

How will I provide recognition?

Appendix B.2   Introducing New Knowledge to Students

Standard(s):_____ Benchmark(s): _____ Learning Goal(s): _____

CRITICAL INPUT EXPERIENCES:

(textbook, video, lecture, demonstration, simulation, Internet, etc.)

Previewing:

(What do you think you know? overt linkages, preview questions, descriptive pattern, teacher summary, teacher prepared notes, KWL chart)

Key vocabulary:

Present information in small chunks:

(student ABC, reciprocal teaching, jigsaw, concept attainment, rule-based summarizing, summary frames [narrative, T-R-I, definition, argumentation, problem or solution, conversation], mental images)

Inferential questions: (refer to *A Handbook for Classroom Instruction That Works,* Marzano et al., 2001a, pp. 270–271)

Represent conclusions:

- **Linguistic:** Notes, write a summary
- **Nonlinguistic:** Graphic organizers (descriptive, time sequence, process/cause-effect, episode, generalization, concept), dramatic enactments, physical representations, pictographs
- **Mnemonic devices:** (symbol/substitute) rhyming peg words, link strategy

Real-life connection:

Students reflect on learning:
- What were you right or wrong about?
- How confident are you about what you have learned?
- What did you do during the experience that you could have done better?

Appendix B.3   Encouraging Students to Practice and/or Deepen Their Understanding

PRACTICE AND/OR DEEPEN UNDERSTANDING OF NEW KNOWLEDGE:

Procedural (The student will be able to):
- Structured practice sessions that are spaced close together
- Practice sessions that are less structured and more varied
- Develop fluency by charting speed and accuracy

and/or

Declarative (The student will understand):
- Identifying Similarities and Differences (Venn diagram, comparison matrix, classifying, metaphors, analogies)
- Identifying errors in thinking (faulty logic, attacks, weak reference, misinformation)

Student Grouping:

Real-life connection	**Homework**	**Encourage students to revise and make corrections in their academic notebooks**
	(Deepen knowledge, enhance fluency, introduce new concepts)	

Student Engagement:

- Academic games (What Is the Question? Name That Category, Talk a Mile a Minute, Classroom Feud, Draw a Picture)
- Inconsequential competition
- Manage questions and response rates (wait time, response cards, choral response, response chaining)
- Physical movement (stand up and stretch, body representations, Give One/Get One, vote with your feet)
- Use appropriate pacing
- Engage students in friendly controversy

Appendix B.4 Encouraging Students to Generate and Test Hypotheses

GENERATE AND TEST HYPOTHESIS ABOUT NEW KNOWLEDGE:

Experimental Inquiry		Decision Making		Problem Solving		Investigation
• Observe phenomenon • Share hypothesis • Collect data • Report conclusions • Explain changes in initial thinking	or	• Identify alternatives • Make prediction • Address criteria by which the alternatives will be judged • Complete decision-making process • Contrast predictions with results	or	• Predict how new context or constraint will affect the situation • Complete task • Restate prediction • Contrast prediction with results • Describe conclusions	or	Historical Definition Projective

Student Grouping:

Plans for enrichment:

Plans for remediation:

References

Bales, R. F. (1953). The equilibrium problem in small groups. In T. Parsons, R. F. Bales, & E. A. Shills (Eds.), *Working papers in the theory of action* (pp. 111–161). Glencoe, IL: Free Press.

Bangert-Drowns, R. L., Kulik, C. C., Kulik, J. A., & Morgan, M. (1991). The instructional effects of feedback in test-like events. *Review of Educational Research, 61*(2), 213–238.

Bannister, R. (2004). *The four-minute mile* (50th anniversary ed.). Guilford, CT: Lyons Press.

Black, P., & Wiliam, D. (1998). Assessment and classroom learning. *Assessment in Education, 5*(1), 7–74.

Bloom, B. S. (1956). *Taxonomy of educational objectives, handbook I: The Cognitive domain.* New York: McKay.

Brookfield, S. (1986). *Understanding and facilitating adult learning.* San Francisco: Jossey-Bass.

Calkins, L., & Martinelli, M. (2006). *Launching the writing workshop (grades 3–5).* Portsmouth, NH: Firsthand/Heinemann.

Calvo-Merino, B., Glaser, D. E., Grezes, J., Passingham, R. E., & Haggard, P. (2005). Action observation and acquired motor skills: An fMRI study with expert dancers. *Cerebral Cortex, 15,* 1243–1249.

Cohen, J. (1988). *Statistical power analysis for the behavioral sciences* (2nd ed.). Hillsdale, NJ: Erlbaum.

Culham, R. (2003). *6 + 1 Traits of writing: The complete guide grades 3 and up: Everything you need to teach and assess student writing with this powerful model.* New York: Scholastic Professional Books.

DuFour, R., & Eaker, R. (1998). *Professional learning communities at work: Best practices for enhancing student achievement.* Alexandria, VA: ASCD.

Editorial Projects in Education. (2007). Diplomas Count 2007: Ready for what? Preparing students for college, careers, and life after high school. *Education Week, 26*(40).

Fullan, M. (1993). *Change forces: Probing the depths of educational reform.* London: Falmer Press.

Fullan, M., & Hargreaves, A. (1996). *What's worth fighting for in your school?* New York: Teachers College Press.

Gerstner, L., Semerad, R., Doyle, D. P., & Johnston, W. (1994). *Reinventing education: Entrepreneurship in America's public schools.* New York: Plume/Penguin.

Glass, G. V., McGaw, B., & Smith, M. L. (1981). *Meta-analysis in social research.* Beverly Hills, CA: Sage.

Glickman, C. D., Gordon, S. P., & Ross-Gordon, J. M. (2004). *Supervision and instructional leadership: A developmental approach* (6th ed.). Boston: Allyn & Bacon/Pearson Education.

Glickman, C. D., & Tamashiro, R. T. (1980). Determining one's beliefs regarding teacher supervision. *Bulletin, 64*(440), 74–81.

Great Source Education Group. (1993). *Daily oral language plus (grade 5).* Gloucester, MA: Wordworks.

Hanushek, E. A. (2003, July). *The simple economics of improved school quality.* New York: The Teaching Commission.

Harvey, S., & Goudvis, A. (2000). *Strategies that work: Teaching comprehension to enhance understanding.* Markham, Ontario: Stenhouse/Pembroke.

Haycock, K. (1998). Good teaching matters . . . a lot. *Thinking K–16, 3*(2), 1–14.

Herzberg, F., Mausner, B., & Snyderman, B. (1959). *The motivation to work.* New York: Wiley.

Hunter, M. (1989). Madeline Hunter in the English classroom. *The English Journal, 78*(5), 16–18.

Iacoboni, M. (2008). *Mirroring people: The new science of how we connect with others.* New York: Farrar, Straus, & Giroux.

Idol, L. (2006). Toward inclusion of special education students in general education: A program evaluation of eight schools. *Remedial and special education, 27*(2), 77–94.

International Association of Athletics Federations. (2009). [Online] Available: http://www.iaaf.org/statistics/records/inout=0/discType=5/disc=MILE/detail

Knowles, M. S. (1972). Innovations in teaching styles and approaches based upon adult learning. *Journal of Education for Social Work, 8*(2), 32–39.

Knowles, M. S. (1980). *The modern practice of adult education: From pedagogy to andragogy* (2nd ed.). Chicago: Association/Follett.

Knowles, M. S. (1984). *Andragogy in action: Applying modern principles of adult learning.* San Francisco: Jossey-Bass.

Lee, J., Grigg, W. S., & Donahue, P. (2007). *The Nation's Report Card: Reading 2007* (NCES 2007-496). National Center for Education Statistics. Washington, DC: U.S. Government Printing Office.

Levin, H., Belfield, C., Muennig, P., & Rouse, C. (2007). *The costs and benefits of an excellent education for all of America's children.* New York: Teachers College Press.

Marzano, R. J. (2003). *What works in schools: Translating research into action.* Alexandria, VA: ASCD.

Marzano, R. J. (2004). *Building background knowledge for academic achievement: Research on what works in schools.* Alexandria, VA: ASCD.

Marzano, R. J. (2007). *The art and science of teaching: A comprehensive framework for effective instruction.* Alexandria, VA: ASCD.

Marzano, R. J., Norford, J. S., Paynter, D. E., Pickering, D. J., & Gaddy, B. B. (2001a). *A handbook for classroom instruction that works.* Alexandria, VA: ASCD.

Marzano, R. J., & Pickering, D. J. (2005). *Building academic vocabulary: Teacher's manual.* Alexandria, VA: ASCD.

Marzano, R. J., Pickering, D. J., & Pollock, J. E. (2001b). *Classroom instruction that works: Research-based strategies for increasing student achievement.* Alexandria, VA: ASCD.

Marzano, R. J., Waters, T., & McNulty, B. A. (2005). *School leadership that works: From research to results.* Alexandria, VA: ASCD.

National Center for Education Statistics. (2002). *Digest of Education Statistics* [Online]. Available: http://www.nces.ed.gov/pubs2003/digest02/tables/dt162.asp

National Center for Education Statistics. (2009). Table 34: Actual and alternative projected numbers for current expenditures and current expenditures per pupil in fall enrollment in public elementary and secondary schools: 1992–93 through 2017–18. [Online]. Available: http://www.nces.ed.gov/pubs2003/digest02/tables/dt162.asp

National Institute for Excellence in Teaching. (2009). [Online]. Available: http://www.talentedteachers.org/action/action.taf?page=faq

Nuthall, G. (1999). The way students learn. Acquiring knowledge from an integrated science and social studies unit. *Elementary School Journal, 99*(4), 303–341.

Nuthall, G., & Alton-Lee, A. (1995). Assessing classroom learning. How students use their knowledge and experience to answer classroom achievement test questions in science and social studies. *American Educational Research Journal, 32*(1), 185–223.

Pearce, N. (2009). *Promethean: Lighting the flame of learning.* [Online]. Available: http://www.prometheanworld.com/

Rovee-Collier, C. (1995). Time windows in cognitive development. *Developmental Psychology, 31*(2), 147–169.

Rupley, W., Logan, J., & Nichols, W. (1998). Vocabulary instruction in a balanced reading program. *The Reading Teacher, 52*(4), 336–346.

Sanders, W. L., & Horn, S. P. (1994). The Tennessee Value-Added Assessment System (TVAAS): Mixed-model methodology in educational assessment. *Journal of Personnel Evaluation in Education, 8,* 299–311.

Schmoker, M. (1999). *Results: The key to continuous improvement.* Alexandria, VA: ASCD.

Schumaker, J. B., & Sheldon, J. B. (1998). *Fundamentals in sentence writing strategy: Teachers' edition.* Lawrence: University of Kansas Press.

Sitton, R. (2006). *Rebecca Sitton's sourcebook for teaching spelling and work skills* (3rd ed.). Scottsdale, AZ: Egger.

Taylor, T. R. (2009). *Curriculum Design for Excellence Inc.* [Online]. Available: http://www.rogertaylor.com

Tomlinson, C. A. (1999). *The differentiated classroom: Responding to the needs of all learners.* Alexandria, VA: ASCD.

U.S. Department of Education. (2001). *Put reading first: The research building blocks for teaching children to read (kindergarten through grade 3).* [Online]. Available: http://www.nifl.gov/publications/publications.html

U.S. Department of Education. (2004a). *The four pillars of No Child Left Behind* [Online]. Available: http://www.ed.gov/nclb/overview/intro/4pillars.html

U.S. Department of Education. (2004b). *A guide to education and No Child Left Behind* [Online]. Available: http://www.ed.gov/nclb/overview/intro/guide/

U.S. Department of Education. (2005). *10 facts about K–12 education funding.* [Online]. Available: http://www.ed.gov/about/overview/fed/10facts/index.html

Vygotsky, L. S. (1978). *Mind and society: The development of higher psychological processes.* Cambridge, MA: Harvard University Press.

Winebrenner, S. (2001). *Teaching gifted kids in the regular classroom: Strategies and techniques every teacher can use to meet the academic needs of the gifted and talented* (revised, expanded, updated ed.). Minneapolis, MN: Free Spirit.

Wise, B. (2008). High schools at the tipping point. *Educational Leadership, 65*(8), 8–13.

Wong, H. K., & Wong, R. T. (2005). *How to be an effective teacher the first days of school.* Mountain View, CA: Wong Publications.

Wright, S. P., Horn, S. P., & Sanders, W. L. (1997). Teacher & classroom context effects on student achievement: Implications for teacher evaluation. *Journal of Personnel Evaluation in Education, 11,* 57–67.

Index

The letter *f* following a
page number denotes a figure.

About the Author

Joseph H. Semadeni is a speaker, consultant, and 4th grade teacher at Osmond Elementary School in Afton, Wyoming. A graduate of Utah State University, Semadeni holds a Master of Education degree as well as an Administrative/Supervisory Certification and is currently enrolled as a doctoral student at the University of Wyoming.

After receiving his administrative certification, Semadeni decided to continue working as a teacher to combine his classroom expertise with his leadership training. This experience resulted in the Fusion model of professional development, which earned him the prestigious Milken Family Foundation National Educator Award in 2005.

Semadeni believes the future of our nation and ultimately the world parallels the fostering of education, values, and learning in today's youth. He involves himself outside the classroom as a Scoutmaster for the Boy Scouts of America and is proud to have earned the rank of Eagle Scout as a youth.

Semadeni and his wife, Gaylyn, have seven children and live in Star Valley, Wyoming. You may reach him at PO Box 1773, Afton, WY 83110 USA; e-mail: jsemadeni@gmail.com.